BOOKS

W9-BNM-775

Perri Klass

Two sweaters for my father

Writing about knitting

A book for my father, Morton Klass, and also for his mother, Millie Klass—my Grandma Mimi, who taught me how to knit.

Table of Contents

Introduction

I love to knit, I love to read, and I love to read about knitting. I treasure the philosophy and the anecdote and the commentary in the knitting books I love—in Elizabeth Zimmermann's *Knitting Without Tears*, in Kaffe Fassett's *Glorious Knitting*, just to name two. I find myself reading these non-project paragraphs over and over, just as I find that I enjoy good writing about food, whether or not it includes recipes—or whether or not I look at the recipes if they're there. Good food writing evokes for me all the pleasures and complications of food and cooking, feeding a family, or chasing exotic adventure. Good knitting writing evokes the dazed excitement of planning a project and choosing yarn, the frustrations of struggling when something doesn't turn out right, the thrill of creation and completion—and also the emotional patterns and tangles that bind us in families. Be warned, then: this book contains no projects. It's just writing about knitting—about how it matters and why it matters, how it fits into life, fits into the times in which we live, connects the knitter with family and friends.

I wish I could say that I only went to medical school to support my knitting habit. It would sound wonderful, but it wouldn't really be true; I went to medical school in part, I suppose, to support my writing habit, and discovered in medicine a new source of stories, a new identity as a writer. It was not my original ambition to be a knitting writer, or a medical writer, either; it was my firm and fervent ambition to be a writer of fiction, and I have been writing stories pretty much ever since I first learned to write. I come of a family of writers, and I think I always understood that fiction writing was a gift, a joy, a labor of love—in other words, that I would need a day job. And thus I found myself in medical school, and when I was in medical school, I started writing about my training and about the experience of being transformed into a doctor. I wrote a series of essays in the *New York Times*—about drawing blood for the first time, about the experience of crying in the hospital. I wrote about having my first baby while in medical school, which was much more unusual back in 1984 than it would be today. I started writing regularly about the fascinations and humiliations of my training, and about medicine and medical issues.

And it was then, as I became something of a "medical writer," that I began to dream of writing about knitting. There was, after all, quite enough medicine and medical school and medical information in my life already. And yes, it might be somewhat therapeutic to come home after an overwhelming day in the hospital and then to sit down and write the story of what had happened, but then, on the other hand, it was much more therapeutic to come home and knit—or to knit at work, if I could get away with it. Why couldn't I write more about knitting, about something I loved, something that helped keep me going, but was in danger of getting squeezed out of my overtired life? All through medical school and internship and residency training in pediatrics, as my knitting habit became more serious, as I became more and more addicted to knitting books and knitting magazines, I tried to convince editors that a knitting story would be more fun, or more exciting, or attract more interest, than a medical story. Nobody bought it—not the idea, not the story. People wanted hard-hitting hospital stories, or, at the very least, searingly honest accounts of the uncertainties and insecurities of turning into a doctor. When I finally got my chance to write my first knitting essay—the first essay in this book—I was just finishing my training as a pediatrician. I had a lot to say about the ways that knitting had mattered to me during those emotionally intense years of taking care of very sick children, those sleep-deprived years of long nights in the hospital.

Now I have been in practice as a pediatrician for more than a decade. The little babies from my first year are finishing up elementary school. The sweaters I knitted for my own first child back in those residency days have been outgrown even by my third child, and carefully packed away. I still write fiction, every chance I get (and I still read fiction, every chance I get), and I still write about the medical world. But to my unending delight, I have also been able to write about knitting, to come back again and again to the endlessly interesting and endlessly complex questions of how our brains and fingers work together, how we move through our lives with yarn and needles, how knitting shapes and colors our days and our daydreams.

Knitters make phenomenal readers. They read carefully and if there's a picture, they sometimes check it with a magnifying glass to see details of yarn and pattern; (a much smaller version of the picture that appears on the cover of this book runs regularly in *Knitter's Magazine* along with my column, and I have had numerous questions from readers about the details of the shawl). Knitters understand, they sympathize, they object, they argue. They are fully engaged with the printed page and with everything it can evoke. It has been a privilege to be part of the knitting discourse. I love to knit, I love to write, and I love to write about knitting.

(Oh, yes, about the shawl—the pattern appeared in *Vogue Knitting*, Winter '92–'93 issue as part of an article by Elizabeth Zimmermann and Meg Swansen, "Artisans and Old Lace." One of the points they made was that you could take doily or placemat or tablecloth patterns and knit them on large needles and have beautiful lace shawls—so this pattern was called "placemat shawl—worked from an old placemat pattern in larger gauge"—the photo in the magazine shows a shawl in a very similar color, but they used a wool/rayon blend and I think mine is part cotton, part chenille—but I have no hope of retrieving details of what yarn I used...the article is on pages 8–9 of the magazine, the pattern itself on page 94....)

I first started writing about medicine for a column in the New York Times, *the Hers column, which dealt from week to week with many different aspects of women's experiences and lives. I wrote about my feelings (often of inadequacy) as a medical student, and about the strange new world in which I had found myself—the hospital. But I kept suggesting that one day, someday, maybe, please, I would like to write one Hers column about knitting. This is that essay; it was published in the* New York Times Magazine, *which at the time ran a regular column every week alternating between "Hers" and "About Men." This was the first piece of writing about knitting that I had ever attempted, and I think it probably gave me greater pleasure, when it appeared, than any other single thing I have ever written. The editor at the Times had obviously been worried that to use the "Hers" space for a column about knitting was somehow letting down the side—retreating into the household-hints spirit of the traditional "women's pages," but in fact this column generated a furious storm of letters, pro and con, which continued to pop up in the magazine for weeks. After this essay was published, it was apparently clipped and circulated widely (in those days before email, when tattered clippings got mailed around). I have, at times, revealed all kinds of personal information in print, as writers do; I have told stories on myself and on my colleagues, I have confessed to many failings and uncertainties. But in writing this piece, I felt that I had truly announced myself to the world, revealed my hidden identity, come out of the closet, and flown my flag.*

A STITCH IN TIME
The New York Times Magazine, April, 1992

"Be very successful in your *public life*," wrote Harold Nicolson. "Fame, more than anything else, enables one to wear comfortable and even becoming clothes." It's a good definition of success. It doesn't work for me personally, though, because in order to aspire to comfortable clothing and authority, you have to be ready to make the gesture of wearing uncomfortable clothing during the years of struggle. And I have regretfully come to the realization that I am not going to learn to wear uncomfortable clothing in my 30s any more than I did in my 20s. The ability to tolerate pantyhose and the ability to drink coffee will remain for me the unattainable badges of adulthood. However, I know exactly how successful I want to be. I want to be so successful, so important, that I can knit at work and no one can tell me not to.

Knitting is my default switch; when nothing else demands my attention, my mind dwells on color combinations and stockinette and seed stitch and the fascinating texture that a little chenille can give. My knitting is very basic: plenty of colors, but simple patterns, simple stitches. And there's a reason for that: I knit at work, I knit at conferences. I need knitting that occupies my fingers, not knitting that requires counting stitches or following complex patterns. But the fascination is still there, the rhythmic lacing of one long piece of wool into all those connected loops, spreading out of one dimension into two, into the thick, intricate, warm stuff that is the prize of handknitting.

When I was an intern in pediatrics, I learned that I could stay awake while sitting still if, and only if, I kept my fingers busy. Every day, they would lecture us on pediatric life support and other subjects relevant to the health and well-being of our patients. And like many other residents, I would sit down, listen for a few minutes, and then gratefully drift off into an uneasy daytime nap. So I learned from the junior residents, one year further along. Several were fiendish knitters. At every conference, there they would be—patterns! Fancy wools! Timidly, I brought in my own knitting. And suddenly I could stay awake.

My mind doesn't wander when I knit. Even before I began medical training, I wasn't very good at listening to other people talk for long periods. My mind easily slips off to make lists, or to plan the menu for next year's Thanksgiving dinner, or, if the hospital atmosphere is not too grisly, to review some well-loved sexual fantasy and spend a few stolen moments happily at play. Over the years, I have written many letters and not a few short stories at lectures and conferences. Knitting occupies that part of my subconscious that otherwise nudges me and points out that I am bored. The two hands tightening and loosening, the catching of the wool again and again, pulling it into the design—this is somehow the right and proper track for me to run along, leaving me free to listen and hear and think.

So when I can, when I don't think I'll get in trouble, when there's someone more senior who's doing it, too, when the auditorium is large, I knit. I can do it in the dark, or at least in that slide-lecture semi-darkness so beloved of those who lecture on Important Medical Topics. And eventually I have colorful and ostentatiously handmade sweaters for my children. There are so many ways in which I regularly and publicly fail in the Demonstrative Parental Devotion steeplechase—the food in the lunch boxes still in the deli containers, the poor attendance at school assemblies—it is a pleasure to have one undeniable trump card, one handicrafty badge of my devotion. Yes, I did. I made that sweater.

But enough about the ends. What I want to know is, when knitting is such an obviously useful, warming, sensible thing for a person to be doing while listening to someone else talk, why is the world full of people who take offense? Why are senior doctors happy to pontificate in front of snoring junior colleagues, but frequently taken aback if a couple of listeners are wide awake and making progress on warm woolen garments? Well, I suppose some non-knitters truly don't believe that we're paying attention. But more than that, I suspect, they're annoyed by the coziness of it, the domestic female associations. My profession, let's face it, is full of senior doctors who are perfectly comfortable with the sight of exhausted, sound-asleep, disheveled, out-of-commission young doctors. That's the way it's supposed to be, that's medicine, that's macho. May I have the first slide please?

One morning last year I was waiting for patients to arrive for a clinic, and I was knitting. The director told me in severe tones that she felt my knitting was "very bad for morale," and that even though there were no patients to be seen, it would be much better for me to be seen doing nothing than to be seen knitting. So I put the knitting away and did nothing. Doctors' knitting violates some tenet of capital-M Medicine.

It is bad for morale because it is seen as a trivial activity, a time filler for people with nothing important to do, an intrusion from the womanly world of home and family. In medicine it is often better to do nothing in a frantically busy, self-important doctorly way than to do something non-doctorly, however constructive, however peaceful, however comforting.

But there are a lot of us out here. Recently I was a participant in a research conference, and I sat and listened to papers I really wanted to hear, but my mind of course kept wandering, and above all it wandered to the lavender wool in my bag. To my joy, someone senior and distinguished took out her needlepoint. I reached for my knitting.

Someday I will be the senior one, the guest of honor, she-who-must-be-obeyed. I have seen doctors in that position commit all manner of remarkable rudenesses. Nasty comments to junior people, grand displays of contempt, brutalizing interrogations of the ignorant. And, of course, they drowse and they doodle and they read and they write. I will not do any of those things. I will be attentive and courteous. But I will be knitting.

A Tale of Two Cities contains one of the more notorious images of knitting—maybe I like it because the regular motion of knitting needles amid scenes of blood and gore actually fits certain images from my own life. But I also like it because I see Madame Defarge's point: if I had to sit for hours and hours at public gatherings in a crowded square, waiting for a few moments of excitement, I would knit, too. What else would there be to do? And then, when the Terror was over, if I and mine still had our necks intact, we would at least have something warm to wrap them in.

And to my delight, that "Hers" column, as it traveled around in knitting circles, attracted the attention of editors at the knitting magazines, and I was invited to go on writing about knitting, and the ways in which it mattered to me. I know very well that I only got that first chance to write about knitting in such a non-knitting place as the New York Times *because I was a curiosity, a young doctor-in-training. On the other hand, knitting was truly important to me all through my medical education, my residency and fellowship training, and on into my career as a pediatrician. Writing about those issues helped me understand some of the connections among the many different things we ask our brains—and our fingers—to do.*

OF PEDIATRICS AND PERSIAN POPPIES
Vogue Knitting, Spring-Summer 1993

Some people, I suppose are taught to knit by their mothers, but often it is a skill which skips a generation. I was taught by my Grandma Mimi, my father's mother, who used a pair of wooden needles and some dark blue wool, and who taught me continental knitting, though she herself came from England. She was not a grandmother who was in the habit of knitting sweaters; her trademarks were dirty jokes and Jewish home cooking. But along with a set of treasured recipes, which I once persuaded her to write out on yellow foolscap ("first, take a nice chicken . . ."), she left me the very unmistakable positioning of the two hands, the feel of the wool wrapped around my left index finger, the sense of tension, control and release, the motion of the stitch.

In high school, I made the occasional scarf. I attempted a blue sweater, but gave up after making the front, depressed by the sense that it was coming out much too tight, bored by all that blue. I took a year off from college in 1976, and spent it hitchhiking around Europe with my boyfriend Larry (the at-the-time obligatory year-off-to-wander-till-you-find-yourself); in Greece, I was suddenly overwhelmed by the desire to knit him a sweater, bought a quantity of heavy white wool, mixed it with some scratchy brown, and produced one of those sweaters which weigh a good 20 pounds—no joke to carry around in a backpack already weighted down with battered paperback books.

And then, when I was in medical school, one spring day in 1983 I got the results of my early pregnancy test: yes, indeed, I was pregnant. I wanted to think of a properly dramatic way to tell Larry, and suddenly it seemed clear to me that this was a moment for the tried and true: I went to the yarn store in Harvard Square and bought some magenta wool and needles and a bootie pattern, went home, settled myself in the big armchair, and was several inches into the first bootie when Larry came home. He stared at me; he didn't get it.

"Guess what I'm doing!" I said, helpfully. Larry's forehead creased. He pondered. "You're knitting me booties!" he said finally, joking.
"Booties," I said, "but not for you," and I watched realization dawn.

As my pregnancy became more obvious, I began knitting in my medical school lectures. I took courage from the young man in my class who was notorious for completing the *New York Times* crossword puzzle each and every day in lecture (we spent hours every day being lectured at and people simply had to find something to do to fill the time). I found that I could make simple baby sweaters and listen at the same time, and I told myself that no lecturer would yell at a pregnant woman busily making a little sweater for an imminent baby. Inevitably, eventually someone did yell at me. Ironically enough, it was a hand surgeon, who felt I could not possibly be paying sufficiently close attention to his lecture on the intricacies of the hand, its complexity of nerves and muscles. I, of course, felt that I was providing a vivid illustration of the hand and its possibilities, but I folded up my knitting and put it away, somewhat abashed.

Also in medical school, since I was now visiting the yarn shop somewhat regularly, I discovered Kaffe Fassett, bought a copy of *Glorious Knitting* and carried it home to

salivate over. I began wondering, in a bewildered sort of way, whether there could be more to knitting for me than just following patterns that were marked as easy.
After medical school comes internship and residency. I started my internship in 1986; I was on my way to becoming a pediatrician, and I was, of course, more tired than I had ever been in my life. We worked all night every third or every fourth night, then all day the next day. And then we went home, where those of us with young children attempted to make up for our absenteeism by spending some creative and energetic quality time with the family, without falling asleep in the middle of it.

Every day at the hospital, we had educational lectures and conferences. The Kidney and What It Does. Shock. Electrolyte Imbalances. Important subjects. We all tried hard to get to those conferences early, because the first arrivals could take the chairs against the wall, so much more convenient for catching the quick nap. I was so tired, so weary and exhausted all the time, that an hour in a darkened room seemed to me to be a perfect, ideal opportunity for blissful sleep—even though I was sitting in an uncomfortable plastic chair, even though beepers were going off all around me, even though a succession of gruesome pathology slides was flashing onto the screen at the front of the room.

I learned that year that knitting could keep me awake, keep me paying attention, keep me sane. I learned this first from watching some of the residents a year or two ahead of me. I once watched a crackerjack pediatrician, someone I admired deeply because of her ability to get an intravenous line into any child, no matter how small, no matter how sick, pull out some fluffy white wool and casually invent a baby sweater for a friend, in the Emergency Room on a slow afternoon. There was another resident who was making an Irish fisherman's sweater which was the most complicated thing I had even seen anyone knit; she offered herself as a consultant for knitting problems, willing to be paged day or night. And so, when I started bringing my own knitting to the hospital, I had role models and also people to turn to for advice, colleagues who would help me decipher a pattern.

I made a sweater for my son, Orlando, then three years old. He chose the design himself, a sweater with a lighthouse on it out of the book, *Maine Woods Woolies*. I was astonished that I was actually able to follow the pattern (and even jazz it up a little; I found myself adding the words TO THE LIGHTHOUSE to the back of the sweater, to make it more interesting to knit). And, even more, I was astonished to discover how emotionally loaded this act was for me: I am never there, I don't see you enough, but I love you and I think about you, and I made you something to keep you warm and cozy. And it even seemed to me that my son understood this; he was eager to go to the yarn store with me and choose wool for his next sweater, and was deeply suspicious of the idea that I might make anything for anyone else. For years I had been telling him that I missed him when I was at the hospital, that I thought about him and talked about him when I had to stay away all night—now it seemed to me that I had found a way to show him how true this was: look what I made you, while I was at the hospital.

Over the years, we have gotten a lot of use out of that book of patterns. My son designed a variation of the "whale sweater"; instead of a solid background for the two black whales, we used a mix of blues and greens and silvers, hoping to suggest the ocean. We tied lengths of all the different colors together, making what my son calls a "magic ball"—this is the method Kaffe Fassett suggests for people knitting his Persian Poppy design, and as he points out, it is ideal for anyone who wants to carry around a many-colored knitting project. For my daughter Josephine, who is obsessed with penguins, I naturally made the penguin sweater—and she is now the right size to wear the lighthouse sweater as well.

Were all the hospital Big Cheeses pleased to look out on the assembled residents and see so many moving needles? Probably not, but pediatrics is essentially a fairly kind and tolerant specialty. And, of course, the residents who were knitting were the residents who were awake, and perhaps some of our lecturers appreciated that attention. Others however, made it clear that they would have preferred us zonked out and snoring; that is, after all, the traditional intern-at-a-lecture posture, and in medicine, the traditional is all. Doctors who wondered aloud whether they had wandered into a sewing circle were letting us know that there was something unprofessionally domestic about all that knitting. But in numbers there was strength, and we kept on.

8

I got brave about using lots of colors, and even, a little bit, about adapting instructions. I was still, however, quite nervous about complex patterns and charts; I worried that if I did anything that involved counting stitches, I would not be able to concentrate on the lecture, the case presentation, the conference. Thus, it was not till the summer of 1992, when I took a long trip with my family, that I dared to attempt not only the Kaffe Fassett magic ball method, but the Persian Poppy design itself. My literary agent, the most glamorous woman I knew, had asked if I would knit her something, and I had become obsessed with the idea of a Persian Poppy scarf, a scarf knitted in the round, so it would essentially be a long tube, orange and red and purple poppies, with yellow centers on a brown and gray background. I thought about this scarf for months, collected a shopping bag full of wool. Finally, the night before we went away, with packing still to be done, letters to be answered, bills to be paid, phone calls to be returned, I sat down and made my magic balls. And now that scarf is knitted right into my memories of the trip; on a Swissair jet crossing the Atlantic, in a hotel room in Hong Kong listening to Larry read bedtime stories to the children, in a van rattling around Java, I was making Persian Poppies. For the very first time, I understood how a geometric pattern takes possession of you, how you stop consulting the chart every stitch because the pattern has its own logic; open wide, fill in the center, close up the flower.

This experience left me eager to try more complex patterns, to overcome once and for all my fear of charts. I imagine myself sitting placidly in hospital Grand Rounds, my lap spread with all manner of fabulous geometric designs, my mind busy with the fascinating trivia of medicine. I will be a venerable gray-haired pediatrician, eventually (surely no lecturer would have the nerve to yell at such a person). I will always remember how much knitting meant to me during what were some of the most difficult and pressured years of my life. I will knit for my children, as they grow, for my friends, and even occasionally for myself. And if I should actually end up knitting for a grandchild or two, I will not rest until I have repaid a little of my debt to fortune, and shown that grandchild how it's done.

This was the first piece I ever wrote for Knitter's Magazine, *which was later to provide me with space to speak regularly on knitting in all its many complexities. When I wrote this essay, I was relatively recently out of my medical training. I was no longer desperately sleep-deprived, though as the mother now of three children, I was certainly often fatigued and disorganized—or perhaps, fatigued by my own disorganization. I was making my way as a pediatrician, and a junior faculty member at the medical school. In other words, I was trying to act like a grownup.*

IN SICKNESS & IN HEALTH
Knitter's Magazine, Fall 1996

I am sitting in a medical school faculty meeting, and we are earnestly discussing some important subject or other. Billing for pediatric visits, perhaps, or the staffing in the emergency room over the past holiday weekend. I am making a sweater for my baby, a soft purple sweater with a simple pink and blue pattern at the front. When I was offered a part-time academic job, the chairman of the Department of Pediatrics told me that I would be expected to come to faculty meetings. "As long as I can knit," I said, thinking it would be as well to get it out on the table, so to speak. He had no problem with that, so here I am, knitting.

And yet, I feel a tiny bit embattled. True, the distinguished general pediatrician beside me is busy correcting proofs of an article; true, the neonatologist to my right is tapping away at his laptop, entering items onto a beautiful graphic of next month's calendar; the developmentalist across the room appears to be playing Hangman with himself on the back of the agenda; and true, one of the division chiefs is obviously indulging in a brief nap. But I am the only one who is publicly, obviously, overtly— well, knitting.

Medical lives are busy, overstressed, and for the most part, full of waiting time, lectured-at time—ideal time for knitting. As a pediatrician, for example, you may stand around and wait while women are in labor, knowing there's something alarming on the fetal heart tracing and they'll call you for the delivery, or knowing twins are coming and they want a pediatrician in the delivery room. It's tense time, preoccupied time—but there's nothing to do but wait. These moments come up often in the hospital—long, tense but boring stretches, with frantic interludes of activity. The emergency room in the middle of the night, the intensive care unit when you're waiting for a transferred patient to arrive.

And the meetings, my God, the meetings. The endless slides, the charts of important data, the printed outlines. Grand Rounds at 8:00 a.m. once a week, the most formal conference on any hospital's calendar. Noon conferences, teaching rounds, M & M's (hospital slang for Morbidity and Mortality conferences, where we go over individual cases). Faculty meetings. Continuing Medical Education lectures. If I didn't knit, I would sleep through them all.

"It's a kind of kinesthetic intelligence," another doctor explained to me once, when we were discussing the way our minds could focus more easily when our hands were busy. I have no idea what she meant, but I value the comment; in medicine, everything is more respectable when it has a scientific name. More than kinesthetic intelligence, however, I sometimes wonder whether this is in fact a form of attention deficit disorder. The cliché among pediatricians is that many of us have thought and behavior patterns in common with our patients with attention deficit disorder; pediatrics, like, for example, bond trading, is a profession full of loud noises and interruptions and bursts of activity. Doing a physical exam on a two-year-old is in no way a contemplative or calm experience; doing it while his four-year-old sister trashes the exam room is more exciting still.

And the truth is, in contemplative, calm situations like lectures or conferences, my mind wanders. And there's something about having my hands busy that tethers it down, keeps me a little more focused. No one who has not experienced this really believes it, and that is why I feel embattled in the faculty meeting, wondering whether everyone around me assumes that I can't possibly be paying attention. That is why I feel compelled to make sprightly comments in every faculty meeting discussion, no matter how removed from my own areas of interest, why I need to ask some penetrating question at every medical conference: Was a urine culture done? Why not? Sure, people may think of me as always running off at the mouth, but at least they'll have to acknowledge that I'm paying attention. In my fondest fantasies, they murmur to each other, why can't she just tend to her knitting?

When I worked in the Newborn Intensive Care Unit, many of the nurses were knitting. In fact, many of them were knitting the same sweater, a black background with insets of bright stained-glass colors. When their impossibly tiny, impossibly sick babies were, for the moment, stable, when all the bloods were drawn and the breathing tubes suctioned and the intravenous medicines administered, the nurses would sit on their high stools beside their patients and put in a few rows on those sweaters. There were times, especially late at night, on the 11 pm to 7 am-shift, when it seemed the only reliably normal, hopeful sign in that strange and overpowering place: babies lying quietly, with women knitting at their bedsides. Surely these babies would live to grow up. Yes, the babies had problems, and yes, those knitting fingers were highly trained to other tasks as well, but it was a small gesture toward normalcy and calm, in the most notoriously strange and stressed place in the hospital.

The impulse to bring pieces of your 'other life' into the workplace is strong for many people. The photos, the plants, the little souvenirs of your hobby. The 'approved' executive themes, like golf and boating, the relics of travel, the crayoned drawings by your children. Some workplaces approve, others restrict, and others prohibit. Hospitals are places that impinge even more on employees' self-expression than most jobs, since people do so much of their work in uniforms. Pediatric residents pin cute little name buttons, featuring bears and bunnies, onto their white coats. Women who work in operating rooms, surgeons or scrub nurses, swathed in scrubs, paper caps on their hair, masks over their mouths and noses, sometimes become famously skilled at eye makeup.

13

To knit at work is to bring more than just the tokens of your other self into your job. It's more than a gesture toward individualism, more than a symbolic ornament on a required uniform. It is, quite frankly, a blurring of the boundaries, a declaration that knitting time exists at work as well as at home, waiting time, listening time, time when the hands would otherwise be idle. If you get me in my more high-flung moments, I will suggest that it is a reaching for spiritual wholeness, a unification of the disparate, sometimes even fractured identities of my life. Right, a knitting together, so to speak. In a less exalted mood, I will only argue that it is a way to soothe myself, to make something useful of all that sitting-down time, to focus my brain, and to produce baby sweaters.

And so I march off on my daily rounds, stethoscope slung round my neck, heavy shoulderbag full of important medical journals I will probably never read slung over one shoulder, and knitting bag, lightest of burdens, over the other. I get to the pediatric ward, and find that the patient I need to see has not come back from CT scan yet, but is expected any minute. So I settle down in the conference room, make a few phone calls. Before the first phone call is over, my knitting has found its way out of its bag, the phone is pressed between my ear and my shoulder, and my fingers are moving. Finish the calls, hang up the phone. Do I fish out an important medical journal? Well, no; another doctor stops by to chat, some patient stuff, some gossip. I keep knitting.

"If I bring in this sweater I'm making, can I get you to help with the part where I messed up?" asks one of the residents. I make no fancy promises; my own knitting is often pretty primitive. I do, however, offer the name of a specialist in pediatric gynecology who I happen to know can answer any knitting question. But by all means, bring it in, I say. The more knitting in the hospital, the better.

And as all the controversy rages about the future of medicine and health policy in this country, I cling to the hope that perhaps the future of medicine includes more knitting at all levels, and a more welcoming attitude toward those who knit. And who knows, this may be more than a daydream. I made it through medical school as the

14

only knitter in my class—or at least, the only knitter-in-class in my class. To my joy, at my alma mater, Harvard Medical School, the knitters are now in the ascendancy— so much that the traditional humorous musical show put on by the second-year medical students in 1996, ten years after I graduated, featured a skit and song about how the medical school, suddenly gone broke, resorts to making its students knit to raise money. All the students knitting on stage in the skit, the director of the show told me proudly, were genuine knitters who were always knitting in class.

Perhaps the day will come when applicants to medical school will be judged on their ability to process complex medical information while performing tasks of manual precision—that is, to knit in lecture. When those who want to be surgeons will be expected to demonstrate the ability to follow intricate diagrams and maintain a high degree of fine motor skill over hours and hours. When those who tend the sick will be honored for their ability to create a soothing atmosphere, and to bring a little bit of the healthy and the normal into the hospital. A golden era will be born: bones knitting on the orthopedic ward, while orthopedic surgeons knit to keep their fingers limber. A child comments, "Look, she has a needle!" and it need not necessarily be a cry of fear. But I'm getting carried away.

So here I sit, in my faculty meeting, making my determined little see-I'm-listening comments. The sweater grows steadily under my fingers. There are all kinds of messages encoded here, I suppose. Yes, I can do this and listen at the same time. No, I don't care if you think it's unprofessional. Thoughts of love directed toward my baby, who will one day wear this sweater, thoughts of mild irritation at those who design the world to be so full of meetings, thoughts of gratitude toward those who design baby sweaters to be simply put together. Everything gets complicated if you tangle it up enough, but every experienced knitter knows how to deal with tangles. You pick away at them, carefully and patiently, you sort out the strands, and then you set to work and make something beautiful.

When Knitter's Magazine *offered me the chance to write regularly about knitting, they made it clear from the beginning that I was completely free to choose my topics—I could start from the issue's theme, or from anywhere else—and free to speak in my own voice. I didn't have to be relentlessly positive, or pretend to any expertise that I didn't actually have, or toe any party line. I could be my frequently crabby and cynical self, knots and all. After this particular column ran, they did get some letters suggesting that I was less than great of soul, and I am happy to acknowledge that the world is full of kinder and more truly generous knitters than I can ever hope to be. Still, I think that writing about gift-giving (for an issue themed around knitted gifts) was a first step for me towards thinking about the ways that knitting links me to the important people in my life, connections that are by no means simple and straightforward, but that turn out to be complex, rich, patterned, and yes, occasionally knotted.*

A GENEROUS SPIRIT
Knitter's Magazine, Summer 2001

My children, sweet innocents that they are, are under the impression that I knit for them because I love them. I mean, I do love them of course, and I enjoy letting them pick out designs and colors for mittens and hats and scarves and sweaters. And yes, I think they appreciate these handmade presents as somehow special. But do they realize, really, that these gifts are aimed only partly at their hands and heads and torsos and necks, and partly at the hearts and minds of the other mommies from their elementary school?

I mean, let's face it. We're all knitters here, right? So let's drop the pretense and admit it: sometimes part of the joy of knitting a special gift for a special someone is the sure and certain knowledge that your handmade gift is going to trump everyone else's store-bought effort, no matter how lavish.

With my kids, I think it comes from that deep reservoir of anxiety about how their teachers and their classmates' parents might judge me. My work schedule is occasionally intense and often irregular, and I am certainly not the first mommy in line when it's time to sign up to chaperone class trips, or to solicit for the silent auction. I tend to drop off early and pick up late, and there are rarely homemade cookies in any lunchbox I have packed. (Don't ask me how some mommies know what's in other children's lunchboxes, but they do—which, if you ask me, is a pretty good sign that these women need serious hobbies, and fast.) But oh, relish the power of the handknit gift: the mittens made to look like bunches of grapes, the wildly striped scarves, the penguin sweater or the lighthouse sweater or the little Elizabeth Zimmermann tomten jacket with duck-shaped buttons up the front.

Oh, the casual matter-of-factness with which I respond to compliments. "Oh, I know it looks complicated with all those colors, but really, it's a very simple pattern." Or perhaps I'll simper, "Oh, goodness, he's going to lose one of those mittens any day now—maybe I better make a third one, just to keep the set intact!" Even when I start out a knitting project with only good intentions—a baby blanket for my brother and his pregnant wife, a sweater for a good friend's baby shower—by the end of the project, I have come to feel some sneaky little pleasure in one-upping everyone else. I mean, there I sit, watching the expectant mother open one elaborately wrapped package after another. Cheerfully oohing and aahing with the rest, and knowing all the while that my slightly lumpy, clearly wrapped-at-home parcel is certain to take the prize. What does this say about my character?

A nicer woman wouldn't think this way. And even I have many nicer moments. Watching my children wearing the things I've made them, for example, thinking happily to myself about their warm little hands, or about the sweaters keeping them cozy through the New England winters. There's no question that I knit love into a gift, looping it into the stitches, working it in with the ends.

There's the gray Icelandic wool cardigan I made for my mother. I swear I made it because it would be soft and warm and give her pleasure. I didn't go into this competing for the best-daughter award, not in the least. But when someone compliments her on the sweater, my mother beams with pleasure and pride, "My daughter made it for me." Come to think of it, she may not be as innocent as she seems. Maybe while I'm subconsciously running the best-daughter race, my mom is actively competing in some other parents-of-grown-up-daughters contest for who has the closest, most loving family ties.

And, for that matter, am I really sure my children are completely innocent here? Maybe it's just pride and pleasure that made my little son point out to his teachers, and the other mommies who sometimes come and visit the kindergarten class (I tell you, these women need hobbies—why aren't they knitting?) that his mom made his grape mittens, but maybe it's something a little more savvy and a little more complex. In other words, maybe it was his entry into the my-mom-loves-me-more-than-your-mom-loves-you competition.

Well, one truth we all know from great literature, world history, our many collective years of therapy, and just plain common sense, is that nothing in families is simple, and very little is pure. We give the gifts we give for an interesting multitude of reasons and motivations, layering love and generosity on competition and possessiveness. Gift making and gift giving are as complex and as fraught with meaning in our society as they are in any tribal culture whose carefully collected artifacts are neatly labeled in the ethnographic museum. So go ahead and label my artifacts, then: these are the needles, these are the patterns, and these are the leftover balls of yarn. The tools, the treasure maps, the husks, the discarded shells, the makings and the leavings of the triumphant finished gifts, which have gone out into the world, carrying me into the lives of people I love—that competitive, small-minded me, that woman who made the gifts, in complex and not entirely good-spirited generosity, perhaps, but in generosity all the same.

19

I wrote this essay right before my 25th college reunion, in honor of the friendship I still cherish with my freshman roommate, the paths we've traveled—and the ways that knitting now connects us. Rather to my surprise, I then went on to spend a substantial chunk of the reunion itself talking about knitting, which turned out to be a link to all sorts of people in the class of 1978—I was going to say, to all sorts of unlikely people, but then, they might say the same about me.

COLLEGE REUNION
Knitter's Magazine, Summer 2003

I got an email from Martha this morning; she had sent me three digital photographs of the baby blanket she just finished knitting, her first serious project after the scarves on which she learned to knit. Martha and I first met in Cambridge, Massachusetts, in the fall of 1974. We were freshman roommates, and we considered one another very exotic—she wrote home that she was living with an earthy New York hippie; I told my friends that they had put me with a valedictorian from southern California whose dress-up clothes were covered with sequins.

But we were friends; as a rooming combination, we worked. We were two girls in two adjoining rooms on an all-female floor of a freshman entryway; there were boys on the first and third floors and girls on the second and fourth. She had the inside room first semester, and then we switched. We went on diets together—and broke them together. We took funny photographs of one another—Martha's family in Orange County had sent her off to the frigid northeast with two matching pairs of fuzzy yellow bunny-rabbit pajamas, complete with feet, and I still have the snapshots of the two of us clowning in matching yellow pajama suits.

We were, we thought, easily the most sophisticated girls on our floor—maybe in the whole dormitory. We felt proudly confident that we would win the prize for most gentlemen callers, not that there was much competition. Oh, we were smug! Oh, we were superior. Once one of the girls next door asked me whether her boyfriend, who was coming up for the weekend, could stay on our floor, because she was worried that if she let him stay in her room, he'd "get the wrong idea." It would be much better if he could stay with us, she said, "because, you know, well, you and Martha, I figured you wouldn't care." We were thrilled with our very mild scarlet-women status, but we told her she'd have to find somewhere else for her boyfriend to stay.

And no, neither of us was doing much knitting. I had knit in high school, and I would knit again in medical school, but college was a kind of hiatus. I'd like to think that I was just too intellectually absorbed to have time for any hobby, but I wonder whether maybe I was just self-conscious. Would knitting have seemed a truly eccentric and peculiar pursuit, as opposed to all the self-styled eccentricities and studied cool affectations I was so eager to adopt? And Martha had never thought of knitting; she took out her creative impulses in decorating her room in a black-and-gold color scheme, with a faux fur bedspread and many small ornamental pillows. My tastes ran more to Indian print bedspreads and spider plants, and we tolerated one another's styles with mutually superior forbearance.

So no, Martha was not a knitter, but she was famous for her typing prowess, which suggests to me now excellent eye-mind-hand coordination and a high tolerance for repetitive finger motions. She had come to college with what was back then the height of communications technology, an electric typewriter, and she typed papers for everyone in the dorm. As it came down to the wire for my required (and therefore resented) expository writing class each week, I would sit at my own manual portable typewriter banging out a first draft, and Martha would snatch the pages, with their crossings-out and corrections and typos, and produce a smooth and perfect copy for me to grab on my way out the door. She also, it must be said in any account of her freshman year, pursued sports-related extracurricular activities, explaining, "Back in my high school, none of the football players would date the valedictorian. But here I am at Harvard and even the football players are smart, and I'm gonna get me a football player!" And she did. I would occasionally walk in on her cuddling with a very very large, very very pink, very very shy young man, who would attempt to hide his rumpled self behind a small ornamental gold pillow. Ah, college!

So we grew up, more or less, Martha and I. We did what we were supposed to do, more or less, we went to business school (Martha) and medical school (me) and we paired up with nice Jewish boys and we had kids. And we stayed in touch; I wasn't at her wedding, because I was two days or so post-partum with my second child, but I was at her 40th birthday party, telling stories about freshman year. I live in Boston and she lives in Kansas City, and twice we met in Chicago, bringing our youngest children, who are very close in age, and doing the town. We see each other several times a year, and we email back and forth about life and work and family, kids and books and writing. One thing we never had in common was, well, knitting. Martha emailed me once that she had met a lady who had told her that I sometimes wrote about knitting—very exotic!

Then, last summer, she wrote to me, "I don't know who else to share this with, so you win! Sarah and I are going to start mother/daughter knitting lessons in August... Sarah has been very interested in knitting, and I have been wanting to learn for a long time. So...here we go!"

And so...there they went. Martha is nothing if not goal-directed, whether it's running a company or going after football players. No surprise, she turned out to be equally driven when it came to relaxing with some knitting; when I saw the first sampler scarf she was making, it was clear she was a total perfectionist about each and every pattern. Her emails began to include updates on her projects—"I am trying a diagonal from that new book you gave me!"

So now, in addition to children and work and families and all the rest, we email back and forth about knitting. About how it fits into life, about how it helps us connect with other women, about trying new patterns and shopping for yarn.

And this morning she sent me photos of the baby blanket she made for a friend, another sampler, with twelve squares in shades of dark pink, salmon, pale green, and ecru; I can see from the digital images that each square is a different pattern, some of them quite sophisticated. I can also see that it is a beautiful and lavish and extravagant gift, a gift of time and attention and beauty.

I suggested to her at one point that she had taken up knitting with a certain, well, lack of casual relaxation, and she wrote back, "Well, you're right about the goal-directed part. Knitting is part relaxation, part obsession. Once I start a project I feel compelled to give it a deadline, with interim deliverables. The baby blanket I am knitting now is "due" before we travel to Boston for the reunion. So I have "budgeted" two rows per day. If I skip a day, then I do four the next."

The friendships that last over decades take interesting turns and twists. There are the people whose lives go in completely different directions from your own, but who remain your windows onto other possibilities—this is what it's like to have no kids, or lots and lots of kids, or to live for travel and adventure, or to settle down in the country. And then there are the friends whose lives keep intersecting yours, sometimes in standard ways—pairing off, giving birth—and then sometimes at the unexpected crossroads. And I guess it's on my mind because, after all, your 25th college reunion is a moment for taking stock of where you've been and what you've done and whom you've become—and, inevitably, a moment for comparing your own life, in various ways, with the lives of the other people who came out of the same starting gate at the same historical instant. I can't tell you how thrilled I am that Martha is a knitter, that we have both, in our trying-to-be-modest-while-trying-to-show-off autobiographies for the 25th reunion book, emphasized the importance of knitting in our lives. I could stretch for a metaphor—about knitting together, or even about stretching—but what I really feel is that despite her sequins and my Indian bedspreads, we recognized each other right away, back in 1974, and that to find ourselves in 2003 both passionate knitters only goes to show the value and the verity of that recognition.

My daughter Josephine, having agreed to be the subject of this essay, will introduce it: "Of all the topics my mother could choose to use for an article about me, knitting— one of my not-so-exciting life failures—probably wouldn't have been my first choice (of course, it wouldn't have been my last choice either, that honor is reserved for "Understanding Your Adolescent Daughter" articles). But it actually didn't turn out to be a story that made me ashamed about being a quitter; it simply helped me realize that while knitting is a perfect activity for my mom, it does not turn out to be a hereditary trait."

TEACH YOUR DAUGHTER TO KNIT: CORRECTING THE MEMORIES, CORRECTING THE MISTAKES
Knitter's Magazine, Spring 2004

My daughter Josephine is in tenth grade, and she hasn't touched her knitting in years and years. And of course I have my comedy routines about life with a teenage daughter (the eye-rolling…the moods…the making me feel I'm the stupidest person in the universe…), and presumably she has her comedy routines about Life With Mother. And I wanted to write about teaching her to knit, but I wanted to write about it honestly—without too much saccharine nostalgia for the child she was, not so long ago, without too much false and self-congratulatory enhancement of my own skills as a mother, and above all, without pretending that the lesson really "took." You mothers of adolescent daughters, I think, will understand that treacherously easy nostalgia for the lost cozy days of uncomplicated hugs, and most will probably also understand the mild trepidation with which I proposed to her, finally, a formal interview.

Do you remember learning to knit?

"I think it was around third grade when you taught me to knit. You would alternate nights when you would teach me to knit and nights when you would read to me, and then when I got good enough you would read and I would knit. I think you were reading Frances Hodgson Burnett, *A Little Princess and The Secret Garden*." (Oh, my God, I had completely forgotten that. I had remembered teaching her to knit, but I had forgotten that it was linked to reading aloud, and certainly to any special books. But the minute she said it, I thought of the beautifully illustrated editions of those two books that I read aloud to her—the wonderful Graham Rust illustrations—and how I wouldn't let her see the movie of *A Little Princess* when it came out until we had finished the book. And I was suffused with a warm glow that was partly nostalgia and partly a sense that hey, guess what, I really was a pretty good mother, wasn't I?)

How did I teach you?

"That little rhyme—under the fence, catch the sheep, back we come, off we leap. That's basically how I would remember how to do it today. You guided my hands— you always cast on for me, and you were always catching my dropped stitches." (And I had forgotten the rhyme. In fact, I began to wonder exactly what memories I was cherishing when I originally thought back on teaching Josephine to knit, since I seemed to have retained no details whatsoever. It made me wonder how many other basic details of my children's growing-up have completely escaped me—how many profound and essential colors and sounds and sensations that must once have seemed precious, unforgettable, and completely characteristic, are now forever out of reach. Yes, there are the details after which I yearn—that precise smell of the silken baby head, remembered with love but never to be recaptured—but how many moments are so unrecognizably lost that I don't even know they're gone? I didn't know whether to get all weepy for my own lost-memory moments, or for Josephine's superior recall— you parents of adolescents will probably understand the impulse that rose in me, instantly suppressed, to say to her, tremulously, 'So you remember the feeling of me guiding your hands—and you remember it fondly?')

The first thing you knit?

"The first thing I knit was a purple and turquoise scarf, and I gave it to my grandmother. I picked the yarn. We used to go to the yarn store, and I liked looking through the yarn and their cards of buttons. I was always a really tight knitter and it didn't build fast enough, it took a very long time to make substantial progress, so you told me to loosen my stitches and then the first part of the scarf looked really tight and the later part looked loose and I was upset by that." (Well, I'm a tight knitter myself, but I do remember that Josephine was unable to allow any slack on the yarn at all. Back and forth she went, with her needles, generating a tiny knot of a scarf, the yarn wearing too deep and sore a groove into the finger around which she had it wrapped. I supplied her with larger needles, and I reminded her every couple of rows to loosen up, and I think she tried. But you are what you are, and I'm not sure you can change your knitting tension any more than you can change your signature—I mean, you can pretend it's something different, something belonging to someone else, for a while, but you know what's really you.)

And then what?

"I knit a few things for my doll's house—I remember a pink striped blanket. But my next real project was that sweater. We looked through this book you got me, *Kids Knitting* and I remember I liked the pattern because it reminded me of a red sweater I had at the time that I liked a lot, curled at sleeves and neck. So I chose the pattern, and we went to the wool store and I looked at all the wools; I knew I wanted to make it striped, I was thinking pink and purple, and I ended up with fuchsia, purple, and bluish violet. I remember we spent some time looking for skeins from the same lot because you told me that they would be closer—the same dye batch. And I started with the back because you told me I was going to like the first part I did least—and sure enough, there were all these little blemishes, there'd be these really loose stitches and things would be a little uneven, I was always dropping stitches, it drove me a little crazy because as you know, I'm a little bit of a perfectionist." (That sweater, now, I remember vividly. She worked on it and worked on it, and, well, it was never finished. That sweater was her knitting career, at once her great and showy success, with three colors and a complicated pattern, and a major garment growing in her third-grade hands, and also her disillusionment. It was that sweater that danced teasingly before my eyes when I wanted to write about teaching my daughter to knit, as if I had taught her not the skill or the joy, but instead all the habits I like least in myself, the overambitious grandiose yarn purchase, the fear of finishing, the bits and pieces left to languish somewhere in a bag.)

What did you like best about knitting?

"I loved picking out yarn and choosing colors and putting together colors. I liked the repetition of the hands, I liked that I could knit and listen to you read—it wasn't exactly multitasking, but it felt productive. And I enjoyed the productive feel of it, doing something with my hands. It made me less restless. Sitting listening to somebody talk or read—I notice it in classes, too; I like to draw or write or make little squiggly lines, I get a little restless when I'm not doing anything but just listening. I liked making things but again, it troubled my soul a little that it wasn't as neat as yours."(I wanted to say, 'Oh, but how could it be as neat as mine, when I've been doing this for decades.' I wanted to say, 'Don't be so hard on yourself, you were getting better and better,' I remember that. I wanted to say, 'Don't be such a perfectionist in life that you can't let yourself learn something new.' And I also wanted to say, 'Oh, I know exactly what you mean about doing something with your hands when you're listening to someone talk. I've always felt that way, and it's part of why I knit, and part of why you should take it up again.' And I didn't say any of these things because I didn't want to break the bubble of the interview, didn't want to change her tone by reminding her of mothers and their tendency to draw moral lessons about life, or even by suggesting to her that we had too much in common.)

When did you stop? Why did you stop?

"I think it directly coincided with you guys not reading to me—maybe when I changed schools and had homework to do and I could read pretty much anything on my own. At a certain point, I put it away in that bag, constantly made resolutions, but I never did it. Maybe my life got busier. I don't like the idea of being defeated, it's very troubling. I've never gotten myself up to attack it again. I think I have a fear of finishing it and not liking it. I do think about it, I think I'd like to knit, but with the amount that the uneven stitching or the little mistakes I made troubled me—I really felt like I'll never wear this, I'm always going to be thinking about that loose stitch over there." (I thought of apologizing—I'm so sorry I stopped reading to you, I hope to hell it was because your life got busier and not because mine did, and isn't it awful that neither of us can quite remember how it happened. I thought of offering whole new projects, new trips to the yarn store, colors to be chosen, practice swatches to be thrown away until her stitches are perfect and even, row after row. I thought of expounding one of those moral lessons about life with a reminder that the little flaws and irregularities of a handmade item are to be cherished. Instead, I nodded a matter-of-fact interviewer's nod, and asked my last question: Can you find that sweater? And she jumped up and left the room, and came back in less than a minute with a bulging plastic bag, opening it up and laying out the pieces of her sweater, looking at them for the first time in more than six years.)

"I still love the colors—I adore the colors—but here we have an example of what I mean—look at these huge stitches! Here are my front and my back—the front looks okay, the back is much bigger, more misshapen—here's one sleeve, I love the curl at the cuff—here's my other sleeve still on the needle—15 stripes on the finished one, 13 on the one on the needles—it looks awfully loose, which is funny considering I started it six years ago! I still adore the way it curls—probably if I saw the finished sweater hanging in this style in a store I would like it, but it's all the little blemishes I know so well that make me agonize over it. It does look better than I remembered it—certainly I didn't remember how lovely the color scheme was." (I watched her stroke the sweater, saw her marveling at her own work. Yes, she was identifying big loose stitches and other small irregularities, but she was also recognizing her own taste, her own skill, her own effort. However she had imagined this sweater—a childish botched project—she was seeing the colors that she herself had recognizably chosen, the lush bulky wool soft to the skin, the intriguingly rolled-up hem and cuffs. I know that feeling, when you look at a long-sidelined project and see again the beauty that originally drew you, and wonder, how could I have let this go after so much work? I took up the unfinished sleeve—abandoned in the middle of a purl row—and finished the row and then the stripe, as if I could somehow alleviate some of the uncertainty and dissatisfaction that had held this garment in suspended animation while Josephine herself grew from third grade to tenth. I could block this, I said. It wouldn't be so hard to finish. And it's so big it would still fit you, or you could give it to someone—you could give it to one of your grandmothers! The colors are beautiful and it's very warm and of course, I did allow myself to say didactically, all your little mistakes will just make it more beautiful. The interview was over and the businesslike interviewer was gone. Could Josephine tell that in fact I was suddenly trying to correct every complicated tension of adolescence, to bring back every lost sweet mother-daughter memory, to teach her every valuable lesson that might spare her pain later on? She smiled at me forbearingly as I worked on the almost-finished sleeve, and she said very kindly, though rather dubiously, "Well, maybe. We can always try and see how it comes out.")

Once upon a time, of course, I too made that first trip to a yarn store to pick out wool. Once upon a time, of course, I also sat and listened to a parent read aloud, and I used my wool to keep my hands busy and help me sit still...

TWO SWEATERS FOR MY FATHER
Knitter's Magazine, Winter 2002

I was very young when I made the first one, probably in seventh or eighth grade. I had done a little knitting and a little crocheting—I had a scarf or two to my name. I used to work on them in the evenings while my father read aloud. And somehow there arose this idea that I would make my father a sweater.

He read aloud to us at night all through my childhood—ambitious lengthy projects (we got all the way through *The Hobbit* and the entire trilogy of *The Lord of the Rings*, back in the late 1960s when it was a fixture on college campuses; I would walk with him across the campus of Columbia University, where he taught, and see students carrying volumes of *Tolkien*, or wearing "Frodo Lives" buttons, and I would feel a grade-school child's sense of pride at being on the inside). He read us volumes of PG Wodehouse, doing the British accents with tremendous enthusiasm, and it is still his voice that I hear when I read Wodehouse. Even as I grew into a somewhat difficult preadolescent, I wanted to be part of those evenings on the couch, along with my younger brother—but I was twitchy, prone to playing with my hair or pulling at stray threads on my clothing, and the knitting was a happy compromise to keep my hands busy without driving everyone else crazy. So I had made my endless scarves, and it was time to take on a new challenge.

Now, Papa was fairly conservative when it came to clothing. No one ever succeeded, not even my mother, in choosing a Father's Day tie for him that he was willing to wear, no matter how conservatively we chose. He liked beautiful things, but they were conservative beautiful things—a Harris tweed jacket, a solid-color shetland wool pullover bought on a trip to Scotland. He wore button-down shirts, with those careful safe striped or solid ties that he chose for himself. No eccentricity, no idiosyncrasy; he dressed like the professor he was. He was not, in short, a man you could easily imagine wearing a middle school kid's first attempt at a handmade sweater.

But my father had great faith. He believed that his children could do anything. When I played the viola, Papa came to recitals and imagined me going on to a career in music (it probably helped that he was himself completely tone-deaf, and therefore unable to hear how ill-suited I, his tone-deaf daughter, was to an instrument where ear matters so much). When I wrote stories, he imagined me going on to publication and success and literary immortality. And when he saw me sitting there working with wool, he thought I could make him a sweater, and a sweater he would be able to wear. And I agreed. I loved the feeling of knitting and crocheting, loved how it helped me sit still and listen, and if Papa wanted a sweater, I was sure it was just a matter of choosing the yarn. And the yarn he chose, of course, was conservative: dark gray 100% wool, wound in those giant dog-biscuit-shaped skeins, a bulge at either end, a center wrapped in shiny black paper. With great importance, I carried home a sack full of skeins, dye lot carefully matched (I think there was a warning on that shiny black label about buying enough wool from the same dye lot to complete your project, and Papa, who began worrying the minute the gas gauge on his car dipped below half full, certainly didn't want me to take any risks. I bought enough wool and more than enough: this was going to be a *major* sweater.)

You know how there are certain projects on which you look back wondering what possessed you? Where you can't understand how this could ever EVER have seemed like a good—or even plausible—idea, and you wonder why on earth you didn't see that before you put in all this work? Well, that is how I feel about my decision to make my father's cardigan sweater by single crochet. I think there must have been a particular pattern in a little booklet of sweaters to knit and crochet, and I remember a black and white photo of a gentleman in an appropriately conservative cardigan, rather small and grainy, but promising a highly suitable garment. I took one look and hitched my wagon to that particular vision, and I started to crochet for all I was worth. I have always been a tight knitter—and crocheter—and I worked with a small hook. The result was a fabric with real, how would you say, body, to it. A material which stood up on its own and claimed its territory. I think it would probably have come in handy on an ill-fated Polar expedition—surely it would have kept out the arctic chill, and in a pinch, perhaps you could have stretched the sweater between two poles and hitched it directly to the sled dogs as a travois to carry a badly frostbitten comrade. As this dense gray matter took form under my fingers, I swelled with pride, and, in my enthusiasm, working my way through skein after skein, I made the sweater longer and longer. I had never really tried to follow a pattern before, never shaped sleeves or armholes, but I muddled along, and learned a certain amount on the first side of the front which I was able to apply to the second side—which was, consequently, a different shape. I did manage to get the sleeves of roughly equal length, but again, in my pride and enthusiasm, I made them very long indeed.

So there you have it. I had created a longer-than-waist-length jacket which looked rather like it was made out of stiff gray corrugated cardboard, and which had high tight armholes, one set differently from the other, and sleeves long enough for an orangutan. It was, without question, a cardigan sweater, of a kind. Did I mention that I had also taught myself to make buttonholes, and that the front band of the sweater clearly reflected my progress in this direction; the second buttonhole was better than the first, and the seventh was really quite respectable.

Why didn't I rip out and redo? Well, I've never been very good about doing that; when it comes to the actual knitting (or crocheting), I am tight and compulsive, but I have this fatal tendency to believe that errors in pattern and shaping will all miraculously stretch into place—or at least into invisibility—when the whole project is put together.

My lap was now blanketed in sweater as I sat on the couch and listened to my father read aloud. Everyone was impressed as the sweater grew, I assumed—my younger brother over on the other end of the couch, my mother, passing through the living room, and most of all, my father. I had created something, well, substantial. Something massive. A monument of a sweater.

I bought fancy silver buttons and sewed them on, and presented my father with his sweater. And god bless him, I do believe he wore it occasionally—I mean, not out of the house (there was no pressing Polar expedition) or where other people might see him, but he did wear it. And that was the first sweater I ever made for anyone—and the first and last crocheted garment I ever made. I went back to knitting scarves on the living room couch, putting down the crochet hook with some relief—my right hand was getting tired.

Well, thirty or so years went by, and I did a lot of knitting. Learned to make sweaters that fit—or at least, to knit for children and aim a little large, and know that eventually the child's growth trajectory would intersect the sweater size. Got much better at little details like appropriate sleeve length, shoulder shaping, and even buttonholes (though I still often find that the last buttonhole on a sweater looks nicer than the first—and I still don't always rip out and redo when I should). A few years ago, I offered to knit my father another sweater, thinking, in part, of that early effort, and of the possibility of setting the balance right by making him something soft and properly shaped out of expensive luxurious yarn.

Papa was enthusiastic, of course. Even when his children were grown up, he still believed we could do anything. His sympathetic imagination followed us along every bend of the career path and into every new adventure, always assuming we had only to decide how to bestow our talents, and the world was ours. If I had wanted to be a molecular geneticist, I would be a molecular genticist. If I had wanted to be surgeon general, I would be surgeon general. So if I wanted to knit him a sweater, the masterpiece would soon be keeping him warm. One weekend when my parents came up to Cambridge, we went to the yarn store, and after tremendous deliberation, Papa found a pattern he liked, for an intricately patterned vest, knit fair isle style in subtle muted colors. Could I knit that, he asked, in wonder at my talents. And of course I said of course, never mind that it was a much finer gauge than I usually knit, never mind that the pattern was singularly ill-suited for the kind of knitting-in-meetings that I usually do. We bought the pattern and the wool and the needles, and I took them home, where they joined a procession of intended projects, a queue of good intentions and impulsive yarn purchases long enough to guide me through the next thirty years, if not longer. Now, I do pick up these projects—or some of them—and I do complete one every now and then, though it's also true that at times I shamelessly bypass this patient waiting group of dear old friends to run off with a new enthusiasm, some exceptionally snazzy yarn or some wildly appealing pattern which has suddenly jumped the line.

But what I'm trying to say here is, I never made Papa that vest. I intended to make it some day, I think—some day when there was a moment for careful patterned knitting. I had the wool carefully put away with notes on Papa's measurements, taken from a favorite vest of his. But I never unpacked the wool and the pattern and the measurements, never made a swatch, never cast on for that vest.

My father died, very suddenly and unexpectedly, in April of 2001. He was healthy, as far as anybody knew, and enjoying his retirement, after forty years of college teaching—he was a cultural anthropologist who studied South Asia and religion and the Caribbean. He had recently published a book and was in the middle of writing two others. He developed a pain in his chest one day, while he and my mother were eating lunch, and then, just like that, he died.

I found myself making lists, sometimes, in the months after his death, of what I regretted most—specific things I had never said, or done, or asked while my father was alive. I made myself balance those lists by itemizing the things I was particularly glad I had said or done—conversations I had had with my father, trips we'd taken, meals we'd eaten.

And I thought about that vest that I never made for Papa. To be honest, it wasn't one of my regrets—maybe I knew, even in the worst of my grief, that that vest was probably unrealistic—that it wasn't really my kind of knitting, that I would have been very unlikely to finish it, even if I had started it. Or maybe I suspected that even if I had started it and finished it, it would never have attained the right fit, the correct and conservative proportions which would have let my father wear it without feeling self-conscious. Or maybe I thought the vest always had more value as a promise to be fulfilled than it could have had as a garment.

I think now about my father and those two sweaters. I have kids of my own, and I think I finally understand both how much you might value a completely unwearable garment which represents the pride and love and effort of your child—and also how you might be able to continue believing, thirty years later, in that same child's ability to make something complicated, perfect, and beautiful. And also, I guess, about the ways that in family life, errors in pattern and shaping really *can* stretch miraculously into place when the whole project is put together.

I haven't seen that gray sweater in decades. When I started thinking about writing this essay, I called my mother and asked her to look through my father's clothing for the sweater, so she could describe it to me and confirm my memory. It took my mother a while to find it, because the gray sweater wasn't where she had thought it would be—in the hall closet where she and my father kept the jackets and clothing they rarely wore. I was sure my father had kept it, perhaps folded away in a box of other arts and crafts projects from my childhood, ceramic ashtrays and hand-drawn wall calendars treasured for their sentimental value. But my parents had sold their house after all the children were grown, and had moved to an apartment. They had thrown away an awful lot of accumulated junk, and put many such boxes in storage. My mother had no very clear memory of the sweater, now more than thirty years old, which she had, of course, not seen my father wearing on a daily basis—or indeed ever. But she kept looking, and finally she called me.

"Guess where I found it?" she said. "It was put away in the bedroom closet—where Papa kept all his very best clothes."

This essay was my little piece of the great general fuss that we all made over the turn of the millennium. It was to be the great defining where-were-you-when-it-happened event of our era, I suppose, with some prophesying computer-crash doom and others planning for the party of a lifetime. I was asked to report on the ways in which knitting was making the great leap forward into the twenty-first century, to talk to representative twenty-first century knitters and sum up the significance of this old craft in this new era. I didn't realize at the time, of course, that a much darker defining event was bearing down upon us, a doom largely unprophesied. When I reread this article, which was published about a year before the September 11th terrorist attacks, I feel a little self-conscious about my own attempts to manufacture a historical moment of change, a millennial before-and-after. But as I think about a new century grown increasingly complex and frightening, I listen again to the voices of the people I interviewed reminding me of the reasons they were carrying their knitting forward, into the uncertainties of the future.

Y2K – THE YEAR 2 KNIT!
Knitter's Magazine, Fall 2000

Well, January 1st has come and gone, with all the attendant millennial partying and millennial hysteria, and as we all know, the computers didn't crash, the water supply didn't fall short, and the space aliens didn't come. We're all fully accustomed to writing those year 2000 dates which seemed so peculiar for the first couple of weeks. And here we sit amidst the new economy, the technoboom, turn-of-the-century angst, and virtual reality, and what are we doing? Well, quite a few of us are knitting, it would seem.

"In a world where everything is becoming less and less tangible—virtual reality, the Web—with knitting you can make something that you need that you can actually use," says Miriam Maltagliati, 28, a New Yorker who owns her own packaging business. I know what she means. I know that in my own life there are certain touchstones, certain moments when tactile reality meets intellectual engagement meets emotional pull. After a morning spent in medical administrative meetings, for example, I start to examine my first patient with almost visceral relief: this is real, this is here, this is now, this baby's body under my hands. I touch, I hold, I think, I feel. That's what knitting does for me. After meetings and conference calls, after time on the Internet and time in the strange never-never land of hotel conference centers, knitting quite distinctly reconnects me. The loop of the wool round my finger and that absolutely distinct combination of motion so familiar you almost can't explain it, with a pattern that requires a little thought and figuring. That irreplaceable feeling of watching something quite literally grow in your hands. And I've never needed it more. So could it be, could it actually be, that in this age of burgeoning technology, booming economy, and easily available mass-produced garments and artifacts of all kinds, this ancient craft can actually hope to be more than a marginal hobby? In fact, there have been lots of signals over the past year that knitting is enjoying a fairly major boom. You've probably seen some of the news stories—celebrity knitters, actresses on movie sets, 7,000 people at the "Knit Out" in New York. There was the New York Times last December ("Knitting's new following includes the stressed out and the fashion conscious") and their long and detailed obituary of Elizabeth Zimmermann. But leaving aside the press coverage, and even the question of which hot actress is knitting what cool sweater, are there truly new and different ways that knitting fits into people's lives as the century turns?

I think about stress. There's always stress—and there was always stress. And there are always pundits to proclaim that there's more stress than there used to be. But there's no question that for many of us, our jobs have expanded out beyond their time slots. I used to stay up late at night and write, and yes it was pressured, but it was also the relief of pressure. Now as I stay up late, I also check my email, and if there's leftover work-related stuff to do, it pops up on my screen and whispers electronic urgency. I've carried a beeper for years, but then, I'm a doctor; nowadays my non-medical colleagues and my patients carry them as well, and we page one another to our cell phones. I am at once reachable and unreachable, accessible by email at any hour, by fax and cell phone and beeper, playing ever more complex games of tag and messaging.

Knitting is here, knitting is now. When I am knitting, I am knitting—no message left, no tracking who owes whom an attempted communication. The yarn travels through my hands, the needles move, and I am creating a something that was not there before. Not a virtual something that can always be altered with a single click, but a real and tangible something, which can only be altered with a heartbreaking rip and then a multitude of clicks. I think about all the jobs nowadays in which there is no something you are making, and even no someone you are really seeing and talking to, and I understand how knitting fits and stretches to fill a need.

John Buscaglia, a New York psychotherapist, keeps his knitting in a special drawer in his office, and finds he can knit in between patients, whenever he has a break. "My work is very stressful," he says. "I find my better days of work are when I have a project here with me." I know what he means; I have carried my knitting through many a hospital day and night. And in addition, he says, the knitting gives him something he needs in his life: "When I don't have a creative outlet, I start feeling blocked and anxious," he says. "It's a good feeling at the end of hard work to have something in your hands." Something beautiful, something unique, something you want to keep handling.

"I buy extremely expensive yarn—when you knit with gorgeous yarn, everything looks fabulous," says Katie Behrens, a financial consultant. I know what she means. I bought my first extremely expensive yarn last year—variegated, hand-dyed stuff. I look down at the patterns it forms and I smile, wherever I am. How come it took me decades of faithful knitting to realize this: I have such limited time; I want the most beautiful colors and textures to work with. The point of knitting for me, knitting now, is not to produce an ordinary sweater for a little less money than it would cost me to

39

buy one—first of all, ordinary sweaters don't cost all that much, and second of all, my time is worth more to me than I can possibly factor. I'm not doing this to save money on basic clothing—that's part of why my grandmother knitted during the second World War, and more power to her—but I'm doing what I do to enhance precious moments of leisure and pleasure time. It's become a real luxury in an overscheduled life—how rare to win points for industry and energy while indulging myself. I look for anything that adds to the sensual pleasure, any yarn that delights my hands and my eyes. And as this new generation of knitters fit this craft into their own overscheduled lives, they look more and more for the delights of extravagant yarn, and they search for unusual patterns—or, in some cases, invent their own, moving from basic knit and purl to designing and creating with a speed that amazes their teachers and the whole knitting world.

Miriam Maltagliati had always wanted to knit, and then a year and a half ago, while working a film editing job that required lots of late hours and "lots of downtime," she took a private knitting lesson and jumped right from the "obligatory scarf" to designing her own complex garments, from hooded sweaters to dresses. "You have to commit," she says. "I've made a major commitment." John Buscaglia also took lessons, in his case to revive a skill he was taught as a child, made one project from a pattern, and then began "designing as I go." He tends to get bored with things once he's mastered them, and inventing the garments himself increased the challenge and also the artistic reward. "People really respond well to the things I have made," he acknowledges. "It's assisted my self-esteem." On the other hand, Tammy Smith, 22, a scientist at a Cambridge, Massachusetts, biotech company called, appropriately enough, Millennium Pharmaceuticals, finds following instructions very attractive. "There's sort of a science to knitting. There are rules. If you do everything right, you get a good product." Since a co-worker taught her to knit, she has helped organize a lunchtime knitting circle at the biotech company, and they have been knitting together for charity. A set of handbags was just donated to the Women's Lunch Place, a Boston charity serving homeless women, and the circle is hard at work on winter mittens and scarves.

Knitting in the biotechnology firm. Knitting in the psychotherapist's office. These are part of the picture of knitting in this new millennium, taking your work with you into all the scenes and settings of life in the year 2000. Miriam Maltagliati knits in coffee shops in New York: "People come up and talk to you and say, 'Oh, I want to do that.'" John Buscaglia knits on airplanes: "As a man knitter you get a lot of different responses. Women start talking to you. Men give you dirty looks."

Knitting can connect you to the people around you, or it can give you a much-needed break from the busy hypercommunicative world. Katie Behrens began to knit seriously during a hard divorce. It offered, she felt, "a sense of closure—I could shut out the rest of the world."

I know what she means. There are times when I am tense or even slightly crazed about something, and I force myself to focus only on getting through the row, only on the progress of the garment. Count the stitches. Count the rows. Call it the zen of knitting. There is no world, there is no project due, there is no airport, no delayed plane, no problem child, sick or troubled. There is yarn and motion, pattern and repetition. It sure beats drink or drugs, and it may even have certain advantages over the new antidepressants—after all, you can't wear them when the weather turns cold. And yes, certainly, there are times in my life when I knit and knit and knit, and find my thoughts turning back to my knitting at the most inappropriate moments (there is nothing like running a Very Important Meeting, and making a little list on your copy of the agenda of the next four projects you have in mind: finish baby sweater with hood; finish blue sweater; pullover for Josephine; afghan). And then there are times when I just don't need it as much, and the projects stay suspended a while—but I always know they're there for me. And that I'll come back and need them again—in 2000, in 2001, and beyond.

So as you bustle forward into the millennium, it seems you may indeed be bringing your knitting bag, well-armed with the new aphorisms of the new knitting. Time is precious—choose your yarn with care. Don't be afraid of making mistakes—if you can design a business, you can design a sweater. In the age of virtual reality, touch something as real as wool, find room in your cyberspace-age life to make something you can touch. And celebrate your manual dexterity in this era of cyberskills; as one avid knitter said to me, "If I can master knitting, I can master a Palm Pilot."

Miriam Maltagliati also sees knitting as a kind of paring down, a craft that even in its complexity and extravagance can yield a simplicity that helps balance your life. "We don't really need all the things we're told we need," she says. "You go out and buy a long string, and with two sticks, you can make something that's personal to you. What a great idea for the year 2000."

But the year 2000 was not, in fact, the year that everything changed. September 11th, 2001, was the day that marked our times, our true before-and-after, the day that our children will write their where-were-you-when essays about—write them, we hope, in a safer more peaceful world. In the days and weeks after the terrorist attacks, I read many very moving personal essays and accounts of the day and its significance. And soon after September 11th, 2001, I was invited to come and speak at the Stitches East knitting conference—and asked to speak, in particular, about knitting in the shadow of September 11th. This is the talk I gave. I took the train from Boston to Philadelphia—I was more tentative about flying in that first month after the attacks, and we were still being told to arrive at the airport hours ahead of time, which seemed foolish for such a short flight. When I got to Philadelphia, I distinctly remember the enormous concrete barriers around the train station and the heavy police presence. Travel felt scary—the people attending the conference felt they were making a statement, committing a small personal act of bravery, coming together in a shadowed time.

KNITTING IN THE SHADOW
Knitter's Magazine, Fall 2002

We know it because we feel it, since what happened on September 11th, but also because they keep telling us so—in everything we read, watch on television, hear on the radio. Everything has changed. In fact, there are moments when you feel a slight sense of the absurd watching people link the subject of the moment to terrorism, and explain sincerely but pompously that everything has changed.

But our lives are different, our country is different, our world is different. We are not living the lives we expected to be living—maybe it would be fairer to say

43

that we are not living in the world we thought we were living in. In that context, as I sat down to write this, I found myself wondering whether I was verging on the absurd myself, trying to write about knitting in the shadow of terrorism.

And yet I found myself thinking of my first text, a letter that someone wrote almost ten years ago, after I had written an essay in the *New York Times Magazine* about knitting at work. To be honest, the editors at the *Times* had been a little wary of my choice of subject, worrying, I guess, that it lacked the larger implications and serious controversies that would have made it worthy of the column inches. So I went out on a limb and promised them controversy. I promised them they'd get lots of letters. And, thank heavens, they did.

I had written querulously about the fact that as a medical student and then as an intern, I often got chaffed, reprimanded, even scolded, for knitting during lectures and seminars, even though it was perfectly acceptable in medical culture for people to come in, sit down, and go to sleep—that was just considered part and parcel of the long hours and stress and sleep deprivation of our schedules.

Why, I asked rhetorically, is it OK to be snoring loudly during a seminar, but not OK to be awake and busy making something warm and useful and even beautiful? I want, I said, to be so successful in my profession that I can knit at work and no one can tell me not to.

Well, they got letters. And more letters. And, thank goodness, some of them were furiously angry. One male doctor wrote in to ask angrily how I would feel if he were busy playing Nintendo during a seminar. Others wrote to complain that there was something trivial, distracting, un-serious about a doctor sitting and knitting at an important medical meeting—but then, thank goodness, there were the people who wrote in to defend me.

The *Times Magazine* ran letters for weeks, first responding to the column, then to the letters attacking the column. My two favorite letters, the ones that came to mind as I started to think about knitting now, knitting after September 11th, were first, a letter remembering Eleanor Roosevelt, in her career at the United Nations, and how she always brought her knitting to meetings. I liked that image.

And then there was a letter from a man who had been a child in London during World War II. He wrote: "My mother was a prolific knitter. During the London blitz, when we would spend nights under fire in air raid shelters, she would knit and knit and knit. I remember one particularly bad night, when a bomb fell close by and I awoke in terror. However, there was my mother, knitting away and smiling at me. To this day, the sight of anyone knitting evokes a sense of security."

A sense of security because I think he could fall asleep feeling sure, this child sleeping in a bomb shelter, that the world would still be there in the morning, as long as she was knitting. Sometimes when you are most worried and most shaken and most scared, it's the little things that matter—or that you remember.

Little acts of kindness and community. You don't knit instead of serving your community, or staying informed, or taking reasonable precautions, or even instead of worrying—but after you've taken your precautions, while you're worrying, you're free to knit. And you know what? It helps. It helps you, and it may help the people around you. It's an expression of creativity and comfort, just as it always is—but at a time when people need creativity and comfort. It's also a gesture of faith in the future and in the continuity of life: we will all be here a good long time, and we will need warm sweaters and colorful blankets and beautiful socks. That child falling asleep in a London bomb shelter knew that as the needles clicked and the knitted fabric formed, the world was holding together more tightly.

There is no question, this is a scary time. We need every light we have to hold back the darkness, and to take proper care of those we love, here and now. They will remember—our children, our patients, our families, our friends, our communities— what helped and what comforted, just as that child in London grew up to remember, and to care enough to write to the newspaper fifty years later.

45

One of the people who died on September 11th, in New York, but not in the World Trade Center attack, was a woman named Alice Trillin. She died of complications of lung cancer she had had back in 1977, for which she had been successfully treated. Four years after her treatment, in 1981, she published an article in the *New England Journal of Medicine*, that sacred organ of my profession's scientific and experimental rigor. Alice Trillin's article, "Of Dragons and Garden Peas," was an unusual article for them to publish, not least because it was written by a patient, not a doctor. I read it first when I was in medical school, and then years later she wrote to me about some articles I had published about medicine—not the knitting article—and we became friends.

She was a brave and lively and most articulate person, and as I was rereading that *NEJM* article, after her death, I was suddenly struck by how profoundly it applied to the terrorist attack, the fears and anxieties we now live with every day, and even, to knitting.

"We are all afraid of dying," she wrote, and she went on to talk about the defense mechanisms that cancer patients construct to cope with the immediacy of this fear—with the dragon. Talismans, she called these defenses, "talismans that we invest with a kind of magic." And she talked about faith in the magic of doctors and medicine—and what to do when medicine fails. About believing in the importance of "the will to live."

And then about what she called "the talisman of the moment," the importance of concentrating on details of everyday life, and taking joy, for example, in being alive to plant her garden peas, and being well enough to care about them.

Here is what she wrote: "As much as I rely on my talismans—my doctors, my will, my husband, my children, and my garden peas—I know that from time to time I will have to confront what Conrad described as 'the horror.' I know that we can—all of us—confront that horror and not be destroyed by it, even, to some extent, be enhanced by it.... It astonishes me that having faced the terror, we continue to live, even to live with a great deal of joy.... We will never kill the dragon.

"But each morning we confront him. Then we give our children breakfast, perhaps put more mulch on the peas, and hope that we can convince the dragon to stay away for a while longer."

Yes, we are all afraid. We are afraid of terrible things happening, we are afraid of having to live and be afraid—for ourselves, for people we love, for our country. And we comfort ourselves with talismans—we also want to believe, need to believe, in the intelligence and the authority and the knowledge of the experts who are protecting us. Even if sometimes they seem less than all-knowing, we're willing to believe and hope and help.

And we take comfort in our will—in our individual will, in our national will, or patriotism, and in our collective will to come together and work together and celebrate together—in a community like this assemblage of knitters, for example. So congratulations on being here and doing what we're doing! Heroism comes on different scales. That mother who knitted her way through the London blitz was heroic, and look what she meant to her frightened child—she held the world together as the bombs were falling.

The world has changed, but there are many worlds, and let us cherish the knitting universe and take comfort and joy in one another.

And finally, yes, what is more the talisman of the moment than knitting, than the familiar but always new and adventurous act of creation and craft. We live in changed times and the dragons are new. But every morning we confront them and give our children breakfast and do our jobs and take pleasure in our friends—and reach for our knitting—and try to hold the world together.

Everything had changed, it seemed—but on the other hand, life went marching on. Flying felt tenuous at first—and then it seemed more or less routine again. But the routines were at least a little bit different. I wrote this essay after what seemed to me a rather absurd airline security experience; the responses I got after it was printed showed me how passionately discussions about knitting on airplanes had been raging in online knitting circles. In fact, the reader responses helped convince me that it was, after all, time to start taking my knitting along once more.

SOMETHING DANGEROUS
Knitter's Magazine, Fall 2002

OK, let's talk about something dangerous, something risky, something out there on the edge. I am thinking, of course, about knitting on airplanes, in this new security-conscious, post-September 11th world. Can you take your knitting in your carry-on? Can you actually whip it out on the plane and soothe your in-flight nerves, or awaken only admiration from the flight attendants with your baby sweater, or just turn those compressed hours into useful rows of even stitches, the way you used to? Are plastic or bamboo needles OK, if metal needles are forbidden? ARE metal needles forbidden at all?

I remember hearing a knitter bring this up, soon after the attacks of September 11th. We were talking about how anxious we all felt about flying, and she said, "I hear they won't let you bring knitting needles on board anymore, either; so there's that comfort gone!" As she said it, it didn't seem like a small or petty complaint, but rather like a representative regret for so many kinds of familiarity and comfort and everyday security, now gone from our lives. And then, of course, there was the joke: Why won't they let you take your knitting on the plane anymore? They're worried about afghans!

Not a very good joke, I admit, but a very pervasive one—I must have heard or read a good ten versions of it.

Now, I like to knit on airplanes—or at any rate, I did. But as I started flying again (as most of us have), I left my knitting home. I soothed my new and stronger flight anxieties with crime novels, celebrity magazines, and the occasional well-timed airline cocktail. I cooperated wholeheartedly (and still do) with all increased security checks—go ahead, x-ray my shoes, check my laptop, search my bag! Glad to see it!

In February, I took a small plane from Boston to Syracuse. I was selected for a random search, and the security agent who checked me was the toughest cookie I have ever faced. After checking each and every one of my ballpoint pens, she got to the two short, polished wooden hairpins holding my hair up in its customary bun. She asked me to remove one, and looked at it dubiously.

"To me, that looks like a knitting needle, only shorter, and knitting needles aren't allowed," she announced. Well, it was *much* shorter—shorter than any one of the ballpoint pens she had just clicked. It had a lavender glass bead at the end for decoration, and it wasn't sharp—which I knew well, since I press it into my scalp every time I put my hair up.

"Um, I think you'd just call it a hairpin," I said, hesitantly. She shook her head. Then she radioed for a supervisor, a tall, serious young man who inspected my hairpins, both of them, and me, with careful attention. Of course, I wasn't looking as respectable as I had at the beginning of the day, since they were checking both pins, and my hair had come down. The young man ruled: my hairpins were forbidden in my hand luggage—or, needless to say, in my hair. Too much like knitting needles.

I was allowed to pack them into my suitcase and check it to my destination, with the two agents standing over me and watching closely to make sure I did as I was told—which I did, reminding myself that I'm grateful for increased security, and suppressing an ignoble urge to say something like, "Do you guys really think I'm going to hijack the puddle-jumper flight to Syracuse with a *hairpin*?"

Anyway, if I hadn't been convinced that knitting on airplanes was out of the question before, that experience certainly made up my mind. But then one day I took a bus trip from Boston to New York, and of course, I brought plenty of knitting—a blueberry baby hat, a baby sweater in a great new variegated superwash wool. I mean, it was supposed to be a five-hour bus trip, and what if we got stuck in traffic somewhere? This is the kind of thinking that makes me carry three extra books and two magazines on every plane trip, no matter how short; and come what may, I was not going to be on this bus without something to knit. So bringing two projects also meant bringing a nice assortment of needles, circular and double-pointed. And needless to say, when the bus got to New York, I still had lots of wool and lots of knitting needles, though I hadn't really made it past the hat.

I then ended up coming back home by air, with my mother, and as we arrived at the airport I thought, "Oh no, here I am getting on the airplane with great suspicious quantities of knitting needles!"

I packed them into my mother's suitcase, thinking we could always check that through—but then there was a flight about to leave, so I grabbed her suitcase and we ran for the gate. The suitcase went through security just fine; but unfortunately, my mother had a little pair of nail scissors in her handbag. She had forgotten all about it, and was stopped and searched. We missed that flight and had to take the next. You know what? Nobody seemed to care about all my knitting needles, not one bit. Made me begin to wonder whether they were actually against the law.

So I called a couple of airlines. At the first, American Airlines, the agent initially told me with complete confidence that knitting needles were forbidden in carry-on luggage. I would have to check them through. I asked her whether she was positive, and she obligingly checked a recent security directive and came back, sounding surprised, to report that in fact, knitting needles are OK, and may now be carried on—after being inspected to make sure they don't contain a prohibited item—along with bowling balls, camcorders, and eyelash curlers, to name a few. Still prohibited, she explained, are bullwhips, automatic weapons, and cattle prods.

51

The person I talked to at Delta was similarly positive, "No knitting needles," he said. "Nothing sharp and metallic," he added, "Nothing with a point on the end like a knitting needle or a crochet needle." (I didn't get into it with him.)

"What about wood or plastic?" I asked. He wasn't sure—he thought it would be at the discretion of the people doing the screening, and he sent me to a particular section of the FAA Web site, which unfortunately, I did not have the computer skills to navigate. I did, however, browse through some knitting-related online discussions of this topic. Most of the postings I read suggested that people had been allowed to bring plastic or wooden circular needles on board, and even to knit with them in-flight, and there were good suggestions about using nail clippers to cut yarn or planning carefully for a stretch of knitting with very little cutting (and of course, leaving your precious heirloom silver scissors safe at home, so you don't awaken the same kind of suspicion that greeted my mother and her little manicure set).

But to be honest, I still don't know. Would I be tense, bringing knitting through security, wondering whether I was going to have to pull the project off the needles? One online posting suggested always carrying a self-addressed stamped envelope so that you could mail your needles back to yourself if they were refused at security. But even if I and my needles got through airport security, would I be comfortable pulling out my knitting on the plane? What if someone objected?

What if someone else felt uncomfortable with my knitting? The truth, for right now, for me, is that I think I have given up knitting on planes. I hope the world gets safer and surer and I find myself once again taking along my knitting for company and comfort, but for right now I'm leaving it home. I support increased airport security; I'm still saying a silent prayer every time I fly that I'll be allowed to keep my hairpins (so far, no one else has objected to them), and I want to assure everyone that difficult as my hair may sometimes be to control, I will never ever resort to either a cattle prod or a bullwhip.

These letters were written for the Rowan Newsletter, *dispatches from the United States meant for a largely British audience. When I wrote the first one, we were, again, still pretty close to September 11th, and there seemed no way to write about any aspect of a national "mood" (if such a thing even exists) without reference to those events. It was also comforting to imagine a larger world community out there, a great wide world of knitters. But then, as more time passed, it seemed possible to write about traveling around the United States—or even about knitting on airplanes—in other terms. Now, I should acknowledge that when you write about "the national mood"—or about "the new millennium"—for a knitting publication, you are under some obligation to "discover" over and over again that knitting is hot, knitting is cool, knitting is now, knitting is new, knitting is forever. On the other hand, there's no question that over the last few years, in the United States at least, knitting really has been booming; that I have gone from feeling I practice a very private craft with a small but dedicated group of devotees to a sense that I am, for once in my life, part of a trend. And to my surprise, writing about knitting has been, for me, a way of writing at least a little bit about the times I have been living through. It isn't exactly a heroic perspective, or even a sophisticated political vision, but it's one way of tracing everyday life in moments of fear, moments of complexity, moments of change.*

LETTERS FROM AMERICA
Rowan Newsletter, 2003, 2004

Summer in the States, and people are on the move. Airports are full, and security lines are long. Families take to the highways, and they cover long distances. It's a chance for long-distance knitting in a very big country, full of long distances to be covered.

I see people knitting in airports again, and on airplanes. I've heard lots and lots of stories about how to get knitting needles through those airport security lines—they *are* technically allowed on planes, but the people at security don't always know it. Bring small bamboo needles only; they don't look like weapons. Bring a project that could survive being slipped off the needles, and a self-addressed stamped envelope with you in case the worst happens, and they won't let you take your needles on the plane. But still, once again I see people knitting to pass that airport time, and knitting in the air as we cover those long distances.

I travel a lot, mostly on business. A year or two ago, I started keeping a life list of states, and I think I've been to all but six of the fifty. Got to go meet with doctors and nurses in both Alaska and Hawaii this year, two big ones outstanding on the list. In fact, since I started keeping the list, the opportunity to cross off another state, to visit one I've never been to, inspires in me the kind of ardor usually seen in a birder who hears a rumor that by getting up at 4 a.m. and hiking for several miles straight uphill and then lying in wait in a particularly bug-infested bit of underbrush, she may add a new species of warbler to her life list. Oh yes, wow, what an opportunity—that's how my heart responds to the possibility of a trip to Montana, say, or to North Dakota.

And when I travel, I seek out the yarn shops. I can tell you exactly where to find good yarn shops in New Orleans or New York, in Nashville and in San Francisco. I remember a long and intense conversation in a southern yarn shop—in a small town in southern Georgia—about what kind of knitting was popular in a very hot climate. The shops are all different, each full of character and personality, each blending local tone and local accent with the very particular aesthetic sensibilities of the individual owner. There is nothing uniform about them, except that they all feel like home.

There is something seductive about the combination of knitting and long distances. It remains my fantasy of the right way to cross the continental United States: a window seat in a jet plane, the landscape unspooling below, from Great Lakes to prairies to Rocky Mountains, and the needles clicking regularly as I knit my way across, working by the natural daylight coming through the airplane window, looking out at regular intervals to check on the changing picture below. Unfortunately, there's often a seatmate struggling silently with me for control of the armrest, glaring at my elbows—or maybe the flight attendants have made me close my shade so that other people can watch the movie—or maybe the security guards wouldn't let my knitting needles on the airplane in the first place, so I had to use my self-addressed stamped envelope…but it's still the right way to cross the country.

And then there's knitting in the car. I knit my way across Wyoming and part of Colorado last summer. I have knit my way up and down the Eastern seaboard on several occasions. I have knit long stretches of the California coast. I have finished my project earlier than I expected, on an anonymous highway somewhere in the South, and ended up in a huge Wal-Mart store, stocking up on the spools of colored cotton cord which were the most appealing yarns they carried, settling back down in the car and starting to knit dishcloths. I have knit the 200-plus miles between New York and Boston more times than I can possibly count—I live in the Boston area, and the rest of my family is in New York, and many a baby hat or child's sweater have I generated on those particular stretches of highway.

I meet fellow knitters at rest stops, or maybe waiting in line for tourist attractions. We identify one another, we click, we comment. You can see across the room—or across the parking lot—a knowledgeable gaze lock in on your knitting. Where are you from? Where did you get that yarn? A stranger stopped to look in my car window at a rest stop in Wyoming and said, you didn't do all that on this one trip did you? Yes, I did, I said proudly. Started the project and started the trip together. Look how far I've come.

When I browse in my own home yarn shop this summer, I hear people talking about what makes a good take-along project. They talk casually about clocking hundreds or even thousands of miles. Some of them are seeing America for their big vacation trips because they're scared to fly, nowadays—or because money is tighter and a driving vacation makes more sense than a flying vacation. And on a driving vacation, you shape your experience of the trip, and your memory of the country through which you drive, by choosing the right knitting project. My own personal private map of the highway between Boston and New York is decorated with colorful hats and sweaters. The long long stretches of brown Wyoming hills are multicolored in my memory with the variegated cotton scarves at which I regularly looked down, alternating scenery and knitting, scenery and knitting.

When the Scandinavian furniture company, Ikea, opened its first store in the United States, they made much of their slogan, telling us over and over that it's a big country and someone's got to furnish it. Well, it is a big country. The distances are long. You can fly over or drive across, you can go as fast as possible to make good time, or you can meander, and you can come home with a new and larger vision of this piece of the world. But as you go, you can keep yourself busy, keep yourself grounded, knit yourself a record of the time that passed and the miles that went by. It is a big country, and I guess what I mean is, somehow you have to knit it together.

I was sitting on an airplane a few months ago with a good friend, and she pulled out her knitting. And since she's a good friend but not a knitter, I was mildly surprised— we've traveled together a lot, and she's sat beside me on many a train or plane while I was knitting and chatting, she's driven many miles with me sitting in the passenger seat busy with my needles, but knitting has always and without exception been my thing, my role, my way of passing the traveling time. I am no proselytizer and I don't particularly seek converts; it's always seemed to me that only some people see knitting projects in progress and feel drawn to them, and those people will surely find their way. I mean, I can walk past fifty artists set up with their easels and sketchbooks in some picturesque part of the world—say, for example, along the canals of Venice—I can see them, all busy with their watercolors or their pencils, richly engaged with the beauty around them, creating little pieces of their own detailed colored vision, and I can walk right past them without my fingers itching. I don't want an easel, or a set of colored pencils—I go right on thinking my own city or touristic or shopping or eating thoughts. So why shouldn't there be people in the world who can sit beside a knitter for hours on end and never wish for yarn and needles of their own? No, I don't proselytize; I look on knitting as my own private interest—or obsession—and I know how burdensome the private obsessions of others can become when they turn into missionary work.

But there was my friend, pulling out her knitting. She had most particularly brought it along on this trip, she said, to show it to me, and to get my advice about something: why was her scarf getting fatter? She hadn't tried to knit in more than twenty-five years, it was something she knew how to do back in high school, but then she happened to be in this store which happened to sell some fancy kinds of yarn, and she came across this gorgeous novelty skein…. Well, no. Actually, what happened first was that she saw this pretty knitted scarf for sale in a clothing store, a light little multicolored thing, and it cost ninety dollars. And she couldn't bring herself to buy it, and when she exclaimed over the cost, the woman in the shop actually said, "You know, you could make that for a lot less!" And then, properly primed, when my friend saw this particular beautiful skein of novelty yarn, it occurred to her that in fact it would knit right up into a very similar scarf—and the skein cost ten bucks!

So she bought the yarn, and the lady in the yarn store cast on for her, and she started knitting, at least in part in a spirit of bargain-hunting hostility: take that with your little ninety dollar scarves! The only problem was, the scarf kept getting fatter—she had started out with twelve stitches, and now, somehow, she had seventeen.

I showed her what she was doing wrong—winding the last stitch of the row the wrong way round the needle, so that she often knit twice into that single last stitch—and I helped her reduce it back to twelve stitches by knitting two together occasionally for the next few rows. In fact, I took the knitting over for a couple of rows, and was enjoying the feel of the novelty yarn quite a bit, when it occurred to me that it was time to pass it back to its owner. But at that point, the flight attendant joined us, perching on the armrest of the aisle seat. She had finished serving a round of beverages, and on the way back down the aisle, she had sighted the scarf in progress. "Oh, I love that yarn!" she exclaimed, and my friend told her the story of the ninety dollar scarf. And in turn, the flight attendant told us about scarves she had made, and while she talked, she handled the skein, as knitters do, admiring its colors and textures. And then she called over another flight attendant, and the four of us talked knitting, and scarves, and overpriced women's clothing for a while.

I asked my friend if she remembered the scene on the airplane, and she told me she remembered it well, and she had been amazed that day—and amazed ever since, when she tried knitting in public. "It attracts attention," she said. "People have opinions and associations!" And they weren't the people she was expecting either; they didn't fit her stereotype of knitters. So, mindful of all the hours I have spent sitting beside her and knitting, I asked her about her stereotype of knitters, and she admitted it was "homey and homespun." People who bake bread, she said. Well, I am not particularly homey or homespun, and I have no bread baking abilities (or even inclinations), but I still knew what she meant in a certain sense—I had found it surprising as well to have those two very efficient women in their uniforms so focused on the knitting—I wasn't astonished to learn they were knitters, but it somehow seemed that they were breaking character, changing the script, when they decided to spend the flight talking knitting with us.

It's been happening to me more often lately, I have to say, that a friend I think of—or thought of—as in the non-knitter category asks me for help casting on—or casting off—or shrinking the ever-fattening scarf. There was something about the craze for novelty yarns and quick little scarves that drew in even the most resolute I-can't-do-that types. Something about the appeal of buying a single skein—or a couple of skeins—of something luxe and exciting and just plain fun to handle, and knitting something without any shaping. I have one friend whose first careful fluffy scarf I watched grow (that was another one of the get-wider-in-the-middle first scarves—and it didn't matter a bit once it was slung round her neck and loosely knotted) who developed a positive addiction and made scarves for everyone she knew. I sat in a room not long ago with four other women, three of them pretty much new to the sport, all five of us just back from a highly self-indulgent trip to a yarn store. The two of us who knew how to knit supervised the other three as best we could, and everyone was making dressy little scarves out of irresistible yarn—variegated, plush, thick, chenille, flagged—you name it. The impulse seemed to be driven almost completely by the yarn, by that shelf appeal of "I am your scarf—buy me—take me home!"

No, something is happening. I may pride myself on not proselytizing, but there are an awful lot of non-knitters converting. Sometimes, nowadays, when I hear airplanes overhead, I picture little interested knots of knitters and spectators, or flight attendants quietly catching up on their knitting (I would prefer that the pilots not be knitting, however, thank you very much—they'll have to catch up when they get home). Sometimes I picture non-knitters, all around the country, picking up those irresistible skeins and handling them and imagining the scarves. And after the scarves, we all know, come the ponchos, the afghans, the sweaters, the socks, the pillows, the shawls, and the jackets. There are a lot of people out there with itchy fingers.

So knitting, in case you haven't heard, is supposed to be highly trendy these days, at least in America. Well, at least in Hollywood. Movie stars while away the time between takes and retakes by working away on scarves to wrap around their swan-like necks and sweaters to skim their sylph-like bodies. And over in New York, hip and chic young women sandwich their knitting in between their killer exercise classes and their aromatherapy-scented facials. For the holidays, my college-age son gave me a knitting kit—needles, yarn, instructions, all packaged up in a hot pink box with cool graphics and a kind of pyramidal shape. He saw it, he said, and he knew I had to have it—even if I didn't make the project (oh, he knows me all too well—me and my unmade projects!). I had to put it on display, he felt, because it was just so, well, cool-looking. And what I say is that if you can package knitting so that a college boy looks at it and feels it would make a cool decorative accessory, then first of all, knitting must indeed be trendy, and second of all, knitting is being effectively packaged—which is, after all, the very essence of being trendy. I mean, this same boy was often, as a young child, dragged along to yarn stores, and while he was quite cooperative about choosing colors for the sweaters I made him, he never looked around the store with what you might call knitter's lust. But knitting has just gotten a lot cooler, that's all there is to it.

There is knitting in the *San Francisco Bay Guardian*, along with the alt.sex.column ("Dear Andrea: I'll be 30 this spring, and after 15 years of an active sex life—straight and lesbian, singles and groups, bondage and 'normal'…trust me, I've tried it all…") is a column titled, "Knitting Ain't for Yer Grandma Anymore." Notice the knitters among us, suggests the columnist: "They look like the rest of us in their hipster thrift shop uniforms, brilliant dyed hair with roots proudly exposed, and facial piercings and tattoos. But they're happy, chatty, relaxed, sporting chic knitwear, and they speak of sock patterns, the perfect cable, and elasticized mohair with such genuine elation that it makes the eyes of the uninitiated roll."

Here on the East Coast, my own hometown Boston newspaper recently ran a long article about the new generation of knitters—"they tend to knit everywhere: on the T, in school, at work, on the beach, in nightclubs, at jury duty, and increasingly, at weekly social gatherings devoted to knitting. And if you think these assemblies are like your grandmother's quilting group, think again."

There are books out there called *Hip to Knit,* or *Stitch 'N Bitch.* On amazon.com you can find a special list, assembled by a reader, called "Beyond Knitting: Hip Chick Crafts." Well, I have to admit, that one made me squirm, and not just because I have absolutely no desire to branch out into tissue paper flowers or pipe cleaner art; I am clearly myself not hip enough to think of what I do as a chick craft. Sorry.

Actually, I love seeing articles in the newspaper about the resurgence of knitting, or about the hip and hot and on-the-cusp people who are taking up their needles. These mentions make me feel that I was ahead of the curve, that I knew something before the smart people knew it, that I can smile wisely at having let the world in on my own smart little secret. And of course, I love the idea that there will be more yarn stores, and more custom for the stores I love, and more books and magazines and patterns. Both of the books I mentioned above were on the holiday list I offered my family (but the hot pink packaging won out). And maybe more than anything else, I love the idea that someone might see me knitting—in a crowded airport lounge, on a bus, in a doctor's waiting room—and wonder whether I am in fact a famous movie star (or perhaps the whole point of being a famous movie star is that you are never in a crowded airport lounge, on a bus, or in a doctor's waiting room).

And yet, I sometimes find myself wondering, where does all this newfound hip hotness (or hot hipness) leave those of us who don't go around in hipster thrift shop uniforms, who lag in the facial-piercings-and-tattoos department? What about those of us who have been happily knitting for decades, thinking of ourselves, always, as creating objects of beauty. In fact, while we're at it, what about yer grandma?

Why children, you know, I wasn't always in my forties. Why, if you can believe it, I was once a young thing myself, knitting my way through medical school. Yes, there I was, knitting in school, not to mention on the T, and everywhere else I could (and yes, indeed, I took my knitting with me when I had jury duty, and if I didn't knit on the beach or in nightclubs, it's only because a medical student's life was sadly deficient in opportunities). And if this aging head can recollect so long ago, there were plenty of other young things around knitting, even in the somewhat specialized world of medical school. And when we got out of medical school and into the hospital, there were so many passionate knitters among the residents that it used to drive one of the program directors crazy—he didn't like it when he looked out into his audience of doctors-in-training and saw so many hard at work on their knitting. There were people in that program who risked their director's displeasure in order to hang on to the knitting projects which kept them calm, kept them sane—and in fact, kept them awake, given the long hours and sleep-deprivation we all endured. Weren't they—we—kind of hip, even way back when? I remember Aran sweaters created during slow hours in the Emergency Room, nurses in the Newborn Intensive Care Unit sitting on high stools beside their tiny patients through the night, working away on complex intarsia patterns. Wasn't that all kind of cool?

And I don't know about you, but I have no desire to deny my grandmother. She taught me to knit, bless her memory, and she knew how to knit not because she was an old

61

lady whose time had passed, but because she had grown up in the early years of the century (in the East End of London, as a matter of fact) at a time when girls learned to knit. She also taught me a number of risqué music hall songs, which she was eager to perform (along with their accompanying suggestive dances) whenever an audience could be assembled, and some jokes which cannot be repeated in print—she would not have been at all fazed by 30-year-olds who feel they have tried it all, though she would probably have felt that those who want to dye their hair should make sure they get the roots as well. And my guess is that what went on at your grandmother's quilting group was probably close indeed to the spirit of "stitch 'n bitch" when all was said and done—and that a great deal was probably said and done.

So let's by all means celebrate any and all signs that knitting, the craft and the art and the pastime, is surging in popularity. Let's celebrate the newcomers who bring new perspectives and new creativity, and the hubbub in the press, which gives us the occasional dizzying sense of riding a sudden and wild wave. But it's only fair to acknowledge the continuity as well—the joy and comfort and creativity that needles and yarn have been bringing for generations, the flexibility and resourcefulness of everyone who has found ways to work knitting into life for decades and indeed centuries gone by. And in that spirit I can welcome with great enthusiasm any number of new knitters—young or old, famous or humdrum, tattooed or unembellished—who are discovering that knitting is, in fact, both very cool and very hot.

The great pleasure of writing regularly for Knitter's Magazine *was the chance to look a little more closely at all the different ways that knitting figures in the lives of knitters—in the brain, in the fingers, in the fantasy life, in the real true life. I would find myself making hasty in-process emendations to a pattern, scribbling cryptic little notes to myself in the margin about the adjustments I had made, and I would think— of course, knitter's arithmetic!*

DOING THE MATH

Knitter's Magazine, Summer 2002

The first few projects I ever attempted, I followed the numbers religiously. Never mind if it was a scarf, never mind if it was obviously coming out narrower than I had wanted it to, the instructions said to cast on 40 stitches, and 40 stitches it was. And okay, the suspiciously narrow scarf was complete (and never mind that it was shorter than I had intended, since instead of giving a specific length, the instructions actually told me how many rows to knit—and, more unbelievably still, I actually counted the rows and stopped when I had the right number). Clearly, it was time to attempt a sweater. I bought robin's-egg blue wool (and that's another story; I don't even like the color, but I have such a clear memory of my high-school self, knitting that never-to-be-worn sweater—why on earth did I choose robin's-egg blue? Had I seen a sweater that color on some other girl and thought it looked good—this was, after all, high school? Or, I wonder now, was the sweater pictured in some similar color on the pattern—I was, after all, in strict instruction-following mode).

Well, you know what the hidden secret was here, of course. As I sat there knitting up my robin's-egg blue wool into the sweater, religiously putting the exactly correct, carefully counted number of stitches into every piece, you know what I was neglecting. It's what every knitting book tells you over and over, from Elizabeth Zimmermann on—gauge, gauge, GAUGE! Oh, sure, I had knitted a swatch back at the beginning, but then, carefully and precisely, I had stretched the swatch this way and that way to convince myself that in fact the right number of stitches with the right number needle gave me the right size swatch. Like I was passing a test or something. And it took me at least those first few projects to learn the lesson: I am a compulsively tight knitter, and everything I do comes out smaller than the pattern says it will.

Now, we won't go into what that says about my character—that's a whole other column, and probably an interesting one, as we attempt to read personality in knitting style, and diagnose psychiatric problems from what we do with our needles. Suffice it to say that my handwriting is also extremely small—what my medical colleagues call "micrographia," and there's no use my protesting that if you only look closely enough, it's quite legible and precise. But never mind that right now; it may take me my whole life to understand why I write so small and knit so tightly (and yet live surrounded by clutter and chaos on all sides)—the fact is, that's the way I knit, and I'm not about to change, so the important lesson I needed to learn was how to correct my knitting patterns. Gauge, gauge, gauge. Well, sort of. I have to admit that in my humble, limited experience, it is not so very easy, no matter how faithfully I try, to take yarn and a range of needles and come up with the appropriate gauge. Everything is always just a little bit off.

And thus, like many knitters, I learned to do three things:
1. Knit loose garments.
2. Always knit everything one size larger than I actually think I need (children, after all, will grow into almost everything—if I'm lucky I'll get around to assembling the garment and working in the ends before they actually outgrow it).
3. Do the math.

I am not particularly frightened of arithmetic. But I have noticed that even knitters who claim to be downright phobic when it comes to numbers still manage to wade bravely into the complex calculations of correcting a knitting pattern. People who would swear they couldn't multiply in their heads the cost of one skein times the eight skeins needed for the sweater, are somehow undaunted by thoughts like, 'Well, I added four stitches to each side of the cardigan front, because I like my cardigans to overlap a little more, and now that means two extra decreases each side at the neck.' Or maybe, 'I'm multiplying everything by one-and-a-half horizontally but keeping it the same vertically, and I've added four pattern repetitions.' The calculations get complicated: the size you think you're knitting, the size that size is supposed to be, the gauge the pattern wants, the gauge you're actually getting. And yet we persist. There's something about the way your mind is engaged when you're really well embarked on a pattern that helps you break down, correct, and redirect its construction, even if you don't think of yourself as particularly inclined in that direction. Maybe that's why knitters so often like to read patterns while looking at pictures of the finished garment—the chance to understand how it's put together, the vicarious pleasure of knowing you could change it around a little if you wanted to. Now, I'm not saying I'm always accurate. I have come to grief more than once with plans like 'multiply everything by one-and-a-half horizontally but keep it the same vertically.' I've made careful calculations, jotted them down on the margins of my pattern, and followed my own stitch counts every bit as religiously as I once followed all printed directions. And you know what? Sometimes my own directions mess me up just as effectively as any all-purpose pattern. But much more embarrassing are the fleeting calculations made in the heat of knitting, not noted anywhere (after all, my hands are busy!), that return to bite me a little later in the project: *how* many stitches did I decide I needed for the sleeve? *What* had I thought would happen up here at the neck? There is perhaps nothing so poignant as the sad recalculating of the ambitious knitter who had assumed that her original arithmetic would be triumphantly, transparently obvious when it came time for the next piece of the sweater.

Knitting is about color and beauty and texture, of course, but it is also about numbers and counting and calculating. I should, of course, invoke Elizabeth Zimmermann once again, and her system for figuring proportions—but I should also invoke every knitter who ever sat down and multiplied the number of stitches she happens to get per inch by the number of inches called for in the pattern (perhaps only calculated by dividing the number of stitches called for in the pattern by the elusive, often unattainable pattern gauge), who ever redrew the pattern, putting in her own numbers, who ever did the math for herself and thereby took possession a little more firmly of her knitting.

Some of these columns were written for specially themed magazine issues—this one for an issue on cables. Writing it, I paged through my Barbara Walker pattern books, admiring the many fabulous complex cables I had never even attempted—and will probably never attempt—and thinking about the minds, cleverer than my own, which were able to invent and imagine those braids and twists and coils.

THE NEXT DIMENSION
Knitter's Magazine, Fall 2001

Cables are the knitter's step into the third dimension. Cables are a jump, a leap, out of one plane and into another—or, if you will, out of plane and into solid. Cables are, perhaps, an expression of some basic yearning for fullness, roundness, ripeness—but perhaps I'm getting a little carried away.

I remember very clearly the moment that I, as a child, understood what the dimensions were. I was listening to my teacher read aloud *A Wrinkle in Time* by Madeleine L'Engle, and she had come to the crucial passage in which the mysterious ladies, Mrs. Who, Mrs. Which, and Mrs. Whatsit, explain to Meg, the reluctant heroine of the book, how it is possible to travel through space and time by 'wrinkling,' folding space up against itself.

"What is the first dimension?"
"Well—a line—"

"Okay. And the second dimension?"
"Well, you'd square the line. A flat square would be in the second dimension."

"And the third?"
"Well, you'd square the second dimension. Then the square wouldn't be flat anymore. It would have a bottom, and sides, and a top."

In the book, they go on to square the third dimension to get to the fourth, and even on to the fifth—but I was left, sitting on the floor, listening to my teacher's voice, with one of those flashes of understanding that you sometimes get as a kid. Suddenly, the world made a different kind of sense: First dimension! Second dimension! Third dimension!

And what is knitting, in its essence, after all, if not squaring the line—the yarn—to get the fabric, making one dimension into two by the intricate connections of loops and twists which themselves probably deserve careful mathematical mapping. Knitting means recognizing the complex possibilities inherent in one long, long line—if it is treated with skill and discipline and a knitter's imagination. The line folds and loops and catches itself again and again until it covers two-dimensional space—in plain stockinette or in the most intricate intarsia. And I know, of course, that there are hundreds and hundreds of textured stitches, giving that second dimension even more complexity and character. Still, to me, cables are something else again: the yarn-wrapped conquest of the third dimension.

I remember my first attempt at a cable. It came while working hard on a 'sampler' sweater for my oldest child. I had marched myself through the various textured patterns, all kinds of combinations of knit and purl, and here it was, suddenly: "Slide 2 to cn, hold in front." Well, I didn't have a cn of course. I had never cabled. I slid 2 to some extra needle I had lying around, and quickly figured out why you might in fact want to be working with a cable needle, and made the always-welcome resolution to go to the yarn store as soon as possible to buy one—and anything else that happened to look useful or important. But it was late at night, and cn or no cn, I wanted to see if I could made a cable appear.

And as it grew under my fingers, with that extra full-size knitting needle flapping around helplessly, sometimes slipping altogether out of the stitches it was supposed to hold, sometimes working its way uselessly in between the two needles I was knitting with, I felt the thick twist of the coil I was creating in wonder: I had conquered space. Along with my first official cable needle, when I finally did get to the yarn store, I bought a knitting book, Barbara Walker's *Charted Knitting Designs* (How many of us, to accompany our yarn stashes, can look with pride on a shelf of books, each a treasure-trove of wonderful intentions—my yarn stash and my shelf of books between them speak of my ambition to live many different lives, take on many different projects), I was especially dazzled by the pages and pages of cable patterns—in fact, the book includes a chart of "80 basic cable crossings." Barbara Walker charted the patterns with her usual thoroughness, classifying them by stitch number (3-over-2 cross, 4-over-4 cross) and by background (all knit versus purl)—but after the exhaustive chart, she did allow herself to promise, "Cables and cable-stitch patterns are endlessly fascinating and endlessly variable." And then she went on to prove it with pages and pages of cables more elaborate than anything I could have imagined— the Baroque Cable, for example, one of her first "nice fancy designs," with multiple crossings and twists, or the almost random-appearing Tangled Ropes, the Saxon Braid with its six strands, or the leafy Fancy Vine. Cables evoked ropes and braids, lattices and gardens, furrows and lianas. And the photographs evoked that third dimension, up-close images of cabled cloth with hills and valleys, shadows and rolling curves. I wish I had taken on some of those designs, at their most complex. I still stop and stare at pictures of sweaters that make particularly clever use of elaborate cable patterns—there is something about the many-stranded complexity, the thin and thick coils of something like the Saxon Braid, which appeals to me deeply. I wonder whether in addition to beauty, in addition to that fascinating depth and thickness, I am drawn to the way that a complex cable illustrates the basic principles of knitting in an almost metaphoric, or perhaps diagrammatic way—or am I getting carried away again? What I mean is, there you have sketched out for you in the form of the cable pattern a picture which is also the essential truth of knitting: order and repetition, twisting and looping, strands that join and twist and separate and then join again to create beauty and pattern and decorate the world.

But the truth is, though I continue to collect the patterns and the books, I have never become a truly dedicated cable knitter. I do have cable needles on hand, and I do attempt the occasional cable design—but not usually the rich, complex braids and coils of my imagination. Part of the problem is my predilection for patterns that can be memorized quickly and followed without consulting instructions—essential for someone who often knits in meetings. Part, I am afraid, is my own weakness when it comes to anything that takes me out into the third dimension; all my life I have been weak at what they call on aptitude tests "spatial reasoning." I can understand and memorize flat patterns, two-dimensional constructs, much more easily.

And yet life is long and there are many projects still to come—that's the deep cosmic significance of the yarn stash and the shelf of pattern books to dream over. Someday there will be an opening in my life for the most elaborate cable project; a simpler moment in life for a more complex charted pattern. And then it will just be a matter of choosing my pattern, my road map out into the third dimension. In *A Wrinkle in Time*, the mysterious ladies explain that thanks to their powers of wrinkling time and space, a straight line is no longer the shortest distance between two points. And suddenly Meg understands, and her picture of the universe changes:

"'I see!' she cried. 'I got it! For just a moment I got it! I can't possibly explain it now, but there for a second, I saw it!'"

And off she goes on her great adventure in time and space.

Much of knitting is technical and tangible, that's a big part of the satisfaction of working with needles and yarn. But you can't forget the importance of dreamlife and fantasy, and the many ways our brains light up around patterns and projects. Without the fantasy—even, sometimes, highly technical fantasies—knitting would not pull us as it does, would not consume our daydreams and lure us along to the next challenge.

NORWEGIAN RHAPSODY
Knitter's Magazine, Spring 2002

Last winter I was in Norway, bumbling around on a pair of cross-country skis and giving the Norwegian children, who apparently know how to ski before they know how to walk, a good giggle. I got out of the way on the trail through the silent forest, and let another family go past me, Mom and an eight-year-old girl whooshing along, Dad skiing without poles so he could hold his toddler son by the shoulders, and let the little boy slide his tiny skis between his father's grown-up tracks. Both parents were wearing serious Nordic ski costumes: knickers and gorgeous, complicated ski sweaters. And the family dog romped along behind, deliriously happy in the snow snow snow. I turned to watch them go, lost my balance, felt my skis slip from under me, and fell down myself in the snow snow snow, but I remember that last sight of them skiing away, a happy blond family under the northern sun.

I wanted the sweaters. I thought about knitting one. I wondered, as I struggled to my feet, whether there was any chance at all that by the act of knitting a really complex, really authentic Nordic sweater, I might myself become someone capable not only of skiing along effortlessly, glorying in a bright winter day, but also the kind of mother who led her children fearlessly out to enjoy the natural world. Could I possibly knit that right into my personality, into my life, into my future? "Kids, follow me!" I imagined myself calling, with a sweeping gesture of the hand holding the ski pole (even in my wildest fantasies, I never imagined myself leaving the ski poles behind to slide gracefully along supporting a toddler). And I must have made a slight sweeping gesture, there and then, because my pole slipped, as I tried to stand, and down I went once again.

When you look at a knitted garment, at a potential project, you start to fantasize. The more alluring the sweater, the shawl, the blanket, the more intense the fantasy. But dedicated knitters know that there are two different kinds of powerful and complementary fantasies that rise up as you contemplate a picture—or a pattern—or something that someone else is wearing.

The first kind of fantasy is far more technical, more tactile, more hands-on. Who among us has not looked admiringly at a friend's sweater, while mentally taking it to pieces—yes, I see, it's made in the round—but how are the sleeves attached? What kind of pockets are those—can I run my fingers admiringly over the intarsia—hmm, but what does the wrong side look like? And we all know the joy of reading knitting patterns and feeling our fingers start to move—anyone who has ever salivated over a recipe knows the slightly ghostly pleasure of instruction-following fantasy. And the truth is, of course, you can whip up ten different imaginary chocolate cakes, relishing the differences in their construction, for every time you actually find yourself cracking eggs and turning on the mixer.

So yes, there is the level of fantasy where you look at a garment, or a set of instructions, and you allow yourself the pleasure of imagining it as your very own project taking shape under your hands. But then, beyond that, there is the level of fantasy in which each garment, each object, brings with it certain trappings of time and place and occupation—the person you would be, the life you would live, if only you had this one particular thing.

We all understand this. It's why the woman in the perfume ad is posed with the hunk—the suggestion is, he's somehow right there in the pricey little bottle. We are attracted to objects both for what they are—their own intrinsic beauty, texture, shape—and for what they promise. And there is no question that knitting something, putting your time and effort and creativity, and not just your money, into this new acquisition carries with it a deeper level of investment and imagining and, yes, fantasy. Fantasy about how you spend your time, about yourself or the person for whom you are knitting—about family life, about work life, about free time.

I made myself a lace shawl once—it took me quite a while, and it was not, when I was done, what you would call flawless. But what sustained me as I made it was not just the intrinsic interest of the pattern, or the beauty of the emerging openwork—it was the image of myself, wrapped in the shawl, sitting in an armchair, reading a book, and drinking a cup of tea. Nothing glamorous, nothing exotic—maybe I know myself too well for that, even in a fantasy, or maybe I was just craving the thing most completely missing from my life right then, a certain self-indulgent serenity. I wanted to be reading a book, all by myself, but not reading a book on the fly, not in some stolen moment—I wanted to be reading in comfort, reading at a moment when I had taken the time to brew tea and wrap myself in a shawl, for warmth and beauty and comfort. I wanted the shawl, yes, but I also wanted a life that held those shawl moments.

And occasionally I admire a knitting pattern for some very sophisticated jacket-like sweater, something that a really well-dressed executive could wear to work and look both original and extremely chic and businesslike, and what I want is to be that executive, with that well-dressed life, instead of the person I am, pushing back the stretched-out sleeves of her cotton turtleneck, before undressing and examining (and maybe getting peed on by) one more baby. I want to be that woman who wears crisp, casual cotton sweaters on her summer weekend days, not T-shirts discarded by her adolescents as insufficiently cool. I want to be that woman on the deck of that ship, cardigan knotted casually around her shoulders. I want to be that mother who thought ahead sufficiently to make (and finish!) a Halloween sweater for her child, all ready to be worn for trick-or-treat.

I have looked at sweaters that evoked for me a life of happy girlfriend lunches in friendly restaurants. At heavy sweaters that suggested time spent romping in the glories of the New England autumn with my red-cheeked children. At sweater

73

sets that would go happily from someone's high-powered afternoon at work to her sophisticated evening out. And as my fingers start to twitch, so does my brain: I want those interludes, that family fun, those invitations. And I let myself believe, for a moment at least, that I can knit something new into my life, if I only follow the instructions carefully.

Knitters see the world through a knitting perspective, of course. We notice yarn shops when we visit a new city. We hone in immediately on the one person knitting in a crowded room. We size up (and occasionally feel up) other people's handmade scarves and sweaters. And when we read novels which we certainly do…

PLOT TWISTS
Knitter's Magazine, Fall 2003

When I read fiction, I watch for knitting. It's not the only thing I watch for, of course—I look out for food and sex and fun, for character and plot and transporting literary moments—but I do watch for knitting. When a fictional character picks up some knitting, the quality of my attention changes; I still follow the story, but some part of me is wondering about the pattern and the stitch and about whether the character's secret thoughts are now partly bound up with stitch counts and pattern repetitions and buttonholes.

Often—perhaps most of the time—that's more knitting thought than the author put into the situation. There are some writers who clearly knew how to knit—from Louisa May Alcott to Barbara Pym, say—and who understand what they are assigning their fictional women when they put knitting needles in their hands, but there are others who set their people knitting because it seems anthropologically or dramatically useful. In other words, it makes sense that this person would be knitting, or it's a logical time and place for someone to pull out her knitting. Thus, the knitting references in *War and Peace*, tracked down by Bishop Richard Rutt in *A History of Hand Knitting*, probably reflect shrewd writerly observation of the times and places when knitting is part of the background business of life—such as servants knitting stockings at sick-beds. And the great genius of Charles Dickens, who created what is probably the most famous—or infamous—knitting image in world literature in *A Tale of Two Cities,* was to put knitting into a scenario—the French Revolution, the

Terror, the guillotine—where it provided a strange and hellish contrast, an ironic, though historically accurate note of dark humor.

But it's more fun when knitting is actually, well, twisted into the plot. I want to talk about mystery novels—in particular, the peculiarly cozy traditional British mysteries that were affectionately described by one of my teachers as "teacake mysteries." He was a very intense, very committed physician, who took care of sick and sometimes dying children, and who made very hard decisions and lived with their consequences all through his workday, and on into the night—and every now and then he liked to sit down and relax with a good teacake mystery, with a vicar and a locked study and a motley collection of suspects, each considerately provided with a plausible motive. It's one of the oddest aspects of murder mysteries, for those of us who read them addictively—that somehow, when all is said and done, they're downright *cozy*. A rainy day, a pot of tea, a rocking chair—and a nice chewy murder. And that, somehow, brings us to knitting. Knitting, after all, conjures those same cozy images—what else might you be doing in that rocking chair on that rainy day? Knitting offers almost too-convenient metaphors for the construction of the well-made teacake murder mystery—following a complex pattern that will be fully revealed at the end, for example, or weaving in all the ends.

I grew up reading Agatha Christie, as you can probably tell. (And you don't have to worry, by the way—I am a conscientious mystery-lover, and I intend to write about these books with care and choose my quotes most punctiliously—there will be no spoilers concealed in this column, no endings given away.) I can still remember the transcendent joy of solving the mystery and getting it right for the first time—it was *The Mirror Crack'd*. I knew from the moment of the murder what had really happened, I saw through the author's—and the murderer's—various little tricks and feints and distractions. I got the method and I got the motive, maybe a hundred pages before anyone in the book did. And I thought at the time (I was probably in my early teens) that I had finally cracked the code, broken through into Dame Agatha's special secret universe, and that from then on, reading her books would be exercises in relishing my superior perspicacity. And then, of course, it was years before I correctly solved another Agatha Christie conundrum.

76

Agatha Christie's star-turn-knitter is, of course, Miss Marple, her old-lady-spinster heroine who lives in a small village, where, it turns out in book after book, she has learned so much about human evil that she can see farther and more clearly than any bumbling policeman. But the police—and other people—persistently underestimate Miss Marple and her sophistication because she seems so much the fluttery elderly lady, carefully shielded from the realities of life. Instead, of course, Miss Marple knows all there is to know about human nature. Let us follow her through *A Caribbean Mystery*—she has, of course, brought her knitting along on her island vacation: "In the course of her duties in a country parish, Jane Marple had acquired quite a comprehensive knowledge of the facts of rural life. She had no urge to talk about them, far less to write about them—but she knew them. Plenty of sex, natural and unnatural. Rape, incest, perversions of all kinds. (Some kinds, indeed, that even the clever young men from Oxford who wrote books didn't seem to have heard about.)" Miss Marple takes full advantage of her disarming old-lady persona. She flutters. She apologizes for her unworldliness. She seems, at times, a little bit confused or distracted. Her conversation wanders, often, into apparently irrelevant stories from her village. And of course, she knits. "Miss Marple was also present. As usual she sat and knitted and listened to what went on, and very occasionally joined in the conversation. When she did so, everyone was surprised because they had usually forgotten that she was there! Evelyn Hillingdon looked at her indulgently and thought that she was a nice old pussy."

Miss Marple's knitting is in no sense fake, in no sense done only for effect, in no sense a cleverly chosen prop—and neither are the other aspects of her nice-old-pussy persona. She really *is* a fluttery old lady, who respects the old-fashioned values and virtues, longs for waltzing rather than more modern dancing, and loves a good gossip. She knows how to supervise a parlor maid (and judge her character) and how to serve tea, and of course she knows how to knit. And you can't help believing that she knits for all the right and obvious reasons—to do something useful with her hands, to pass the time, to produce warm and useful objects to be given to friends and family—but you also know that her knitting needles are part of her detective armamentarium. She knits when she's detecting—to keep people talking in her presence, while she disappears into the background, as in the above scene. She knits when she's preventing a murder—if Miss Marple is sitting at a bedside and keeping a sick person company, it's probably because she's afraid that person is the object of someone's homicidal intentions. "Miss Marple checked her knitting requirements, saw that she had all she wanted with her.... 'I'm all right,' said Molly. 'Quite all right. Just—oh, just sleepy.' 'I shan't talk,' said Miss Marple. 'You just lie quiet and rest. I'll get on with my knitting.' "

And finally, in this particular mystery, when the moment of truth arrives, and she must act to catch the killer, she wraps herself up warmly (the night air, even in the Caribbean, can be chilly for an elderly lady, after all) in "a fluffy scarf of pale pink wool," which we must assume is the product of all that industrious knitting, and goes into battle. And it seems only fitting that after her knitting has carried her through the investigation, and helped her safeguard a possible victim, she should wrap herself in a pale pink and fluffy knitted garment as she goes off to confront evil. The scarf, after all, we might imagine, is rather like Miss Marple herself: feminine and traditional and even maybe just a tiny bit ditsy to look at, but strong, well-constructed, warm, and highly serviceable.

Knitting goes perfectly, in so many ways, with books that are themselves constructed as sophisticated puzzles, complex patterns full of twists and turns. When you come to the end of such a novel, you look back and appreciate all the most elaborate zigs and zags, all the places where the pattern turned inside out, or where the individual twists suddenly wove together into a remarkable braid that you hadn't been expecting. No, Miss Marple's knitting is not fake. It's part of who she is, and she presses it into service as she detects. In the same way, gossip is part of who she is, and her gossip skills help her tease out one murder after another. And somehow the gossip and the knitting enhance the teacake mystery, with its odd mix of domesticity and bloodthirstiness, its comforting certainty that yes, human nature is evil and murder is common (Miss Marple comes across murders everywhere she goes, needless to say), but on the other hand, all problems have solutions and all mysteries can ultimately be explained.

Perhaps the wisest statement on knitting and the teacake mystery was made by Lord Peter Wimsey, not himself a knitter, but the dashing aristocratic hero of Dorothy L. Sayers' series of murder mysteries. Lord Peter, it happens, has a very shrewd and very reliable assistant he employs when he needs certain kinds of delicate investigations done. Her name is Miss Climpson, and she is very much in the Marple mode—she is introduced (in *Unnatural Death*) as "a thin, middle-aged woman, with a sharp, sallow face and very vivacious manner…her iron-gray hair was dressed under a net, in the style fashionable in the reign of the late King Edward." She appears in a number of the Dorothy L. Sayers mysteries, and proves herself intelligent, dogged, inventive, and profoundly courageous. And she can do what Lord Peter cannot. As he explains to his Scotland Yard friend, "People want questions asked. Whom do they send? A man with large flat feet and a notebook—the sort of man whose private life is conducted in a series of inarticulate grunts. I send a lady with a long, woolly jumper on knitting-needles and jingly things round her neck. Of course she asks questions—everyone expects it. Nobody is surprised. Nobody is alarmed."

I keep coming back to knitting and travel. Whether it's airport security or the joy of fantasizing about foreign sweaters, or the fear of running out of wool on a long bus ride, I keep coming back to knitting and travel....

TRAVELING STITCHES
Knitter's Magazine, Summer 2004

I keep wondering about the connections between knitting and travel. I mean, in certain ways you might think they were almost opposite images, with knitting an archetypal stay-at-home domestic activity, the antithesis of footloose wandering, adventure, or even plain old going out. Remember the song "Cabaret" from the musical: "Put down the knitting, the book, and the broom, it's time for a holiday...."

But the truth is, though knitting still carries at least some cozy connotations of staying home (in the rocking chair? by the fireside?) and keeping busy, many of us wouldn't dream, as the advertisement says, of leaving home without it. I spend as much time before a trip calculating my knitting preparations as I do calculating my clothing—and sometimes more, which, of course, may not say much for my level of rumpled suitcase fashion when in transit. But I know that when I write about knitting, stories about specific projects I was making on specific trips keep coming to mind—I remember the knitting more vividly when it took place in an exotic setting.

When I was 19 years old, I took a year off from college and spent 14 months traveling around Europe with my boyfriend. I knew how to knit—I had knit in high school—but I hadn't done any knitting for a couple of years. When we got to Greece, in the spring, I looked at the various handknit sweaters for sale in the souvenir shops, and I became suddenly desperate for wool and needles. On our very very tight budget (think backpacks, think little tent, think constantly searching out other English-speaking travelers in the hope of trading paperback books because we couldn't afford to buy them new), I somehow managed to acquire a large amount of rather scratchy and, to put it mildly, not highly processed, brown and white wool, and a set of circular needles, and I declared my intention of knitting Larry a sweater.

Our budget was limited, and so was our packing space. I carried the wool and needles around in my backpack (there was room for a few battered paperback books as well, and not much else) and I knitted around and around and around and around on my circular needles as we traveled through Greece, took the ferry over to Italy, and crawled slowly up the boot. I can't remember whether I ever actually finished the sweater—by the time it even approached completion, we were getting close to the Mediterranean summer, and Larry was highly unlikely to need a thick, scratchy, brown and white sweater. It had become too hot to work comfortably with the wool, especially sitting outside in a hot campground, and my temporary mania had passed; we mailed the sweater home in a box we sent from (I think) Spain, and it is probably still packed among our many souvenirs from that wandering year.

So yes, of course, I can't imagine a long car trip without knitting. Or a long train trip, or a long bus trip. Give me a knitting project and I actually look forward to time in motion; take my knitting away and I start to twitch. But that's not the whole story. And yes, of course, knitting helps me when I'm tense, which covers many travel scenarios, from time in the car with my children fighting in the back seat to airport delays. But that's not the whole story.

What I have come to realize is that knitting while I travel is taking a small but very important part of my life along with me, that it allows me to inhabit a new city or a new country in a different way. Yes, I am just passing through. Yes, I am a tourist. Yes, I have no real business here. But I am also doing something real, something that is part of my life back home, something that anchors me in myself and also connects me to my setting. When I sit on a bench in a park in a foreign city and work on a scarf, or a sock, or a baby sweater, I am staking a kind of claim: I am occupying this space, here and now, and not just passing through. By knitting in a foreign place, I feel I am, just briefly, living in that place, breathing in the air as my fingers move; living there as myself, with my preferences and my habits and my peculiarities.

The best analogy, come to think of it (and remembering those battered paperback books in that backpack all those years ago) is probably reading. I also obsess over what books to bring, before I go on any trip, and I worry about running out of books with the same kind of anxiety that makes me throw a second knitting project into my bag before a long drive: wouldn't it be terrible if I came to the end and still had hours and hours of time left ahead of me? When I was 19, traveling around with my backpack, we couldn't really afford to buy new English books (even before I spent all our extra drachmas on wool), so we relied on coming across other travelers (usually also with backpacks) who had books to trade. Unfortunately, just about every single English-speaking traveler in Europe that year was reading the same book, *Centennial*, by James Michener (that's what you get for starting your big trip in 1976), and after I had read it, I had to keep turning down new copies—and other pickings were often slim. So every now and then I would allow myself to splurge on whatever was the thickest, likely-to-last-the-longest English book available in the English-language section of the biggest bookstore in whatever city we were in. That was the year I read *War and Peace*, and *Moby Dick,* not to mention *Tristram Shandy,* all carefully selected by number of pages. But reading was more than just distraction, I think. It was another way of occupying air and space in foreign countries that somehow made them *mine*: in addition to tourist activities, in addition to sightseeing, and hunting for accommodations (and I got very good at asking, 'Do you know where the camping place is?' in many languages), and negotiating transport, by sitting and reading in a park, or a campsite, or a bus station, or outside some famous tourist sight, or even inside some famous tourist sight, you make it a little bit your own.

So that's the connection, I think, between knitting and traveling. By bringing your domesticity with you, by bringing along something that connects you both spiritually and practically with who you are at home, you effect a subtle change in the way that you breathe alien air. And then you bring home something that was made, in part, in that alien air, that carries, worked into its stitches, the place you were and the sights you saw and the thoughts you thought while you moved your needles. Knitting is a way of saying what I still say to myself when I find myself somewhere unexpected, somewhere exotic, someplace beautiful: Look where I am! Look where I've gotten to!

The last big trip I made was to southern Spain, to Andalusia, with Larry and our eight-year-old son. Larry and I haven't been there since that visit in 1977, toward the end of that long, mid-college wander year. We were both getting pretty tired, by the time we got to Spain; our backpacks were worn and grimy and so were we, I suppose. I don't remember everything we saw and did, but I remember the Alhambra, the spectacular Moorish palace of the last Islamic kingdom in Spain. The Alhambra is in Granada, the last Spanish city to fall to the Catholic reconquest; it was taken by Ferdinand and Isabella in 1492. Back when we were 19, we wandered around and admired the dazzling decorated rooms and the courtyards and fountains—and then, of course, we settled down to read for a while in the terraced gardens. And I thought, of course, that I would have to come back. And 27 years later, so I did—somewhat less grubby, and without a backpack, though in other ways perhaps the worse for wear. And the Alhambra is still dazzling, and it's still a pleasure to settle down in the gardens and read, and listen to the fountains. The day after our visit to the Alhambra itself, we spent the afternoon walking around the town of Granada. We climbed a hill and looked across at the Alhambra, at the dramatic red building high above the city, and tried to point out to our son the various towers and structures we had visited the day before. And then we sat down in a garden (actually, in the garden of a new mosque, the first mosque to be built in Granada since 1492!), and Larry and our son took out their books—and I took out my knitting. I looked across the valley at the Alhambra on its hillside, and I worked on my scarf (two yarns together, one flat cotton ribbon, one variegated fancy chenille), I moved my needles and I took deep breaths and I told myself, look where I am! That is the Alhambra, and here I am, and this, I suppose, is my Alhambra scarf. I'll work on it here, and then I'll bring it back home.

But travel, you know, is not all external. There are also the voyages of the mind, geographical, spiritual, metaphysical, or just plain wistful.

KNITTING FANTASIES
Knitter's Magazine, Winter 2003

So I went, for the first time in my life, on a cruise of sorts, a trip in a small sailing ship from Dubrovnik to Venice. And before I left, never having been on a cruise, I found I had two recurrent fantasies, two images that came to mind whenever I thought about the trip. In one, I was reclining on deck, in a deck chair, reading novel after novel as the sun glinted on the water and the heavily wooded coast of Dalmatia slipped past. In the other, of course, I was knitting. My luggage for the trip was strongly biased toward books and yarn, and imagine, if you will, with what a sense of triumph I scored my deck chair, sat down in the Adriatic sun, and pulled out my knitting. I had made the picture come true; there were the great white sails above me, there was the salt wind in my hair, there went the boat among the islands, there I sat, able to appreciate the setting and the motion because I had achieved the perfect position, with needles satisfyingly firm in my hands and a shawl growing out of my lap and onto the deck chair.

Before getting ready for this trip, I had no idea that the knitting-on-deck fantasy was so vivid and potent and ready to hand. But as a devoted knitter of the keep-my-hands-busy-while-I-do-something-else school, I do tend to develop the occasional specific, powerful desire, half lifestyle ambition, half finger-flexing fantasy of a real-life activity, a particular set of moments that could be completed and ennobled by knitting.

The boat-deck fantasy was perfectly permissable; it was only out of reach because of the circumstances of my life—if I were someone who went cruising every year, then there would have been nothing notable about knitting on deck. And maybe there are other situational fantasies waiting to surprise me when life presents the opportunity. (Do I dream of knitting in an alpine ski resort? Well, no, I don't think so—but maybe because, as a nonskier, that would be the only physical activity available to me, making that particular vacation choice highly unlikely.) But generally, I find, these fantasies refer to moments when for one reason or another—social mores, artistic pretensions, common courtesy—I don't think I can claim the right to pull out my knitting. And thus I am left to yearn, to cherish my private images, and perhaps, every now and then, to achieve a special case, a hint of the bliss that could be.

For example, I have felt for years that classical music would be enhanced by knitting. I know, I know, the needles might click, even the whisper of yarn against yarn would be enough to upset some music lovers. I have no intention of pulling out my knitting at the symphony. I just know that if I only could, I might have a chance of reliably achieving that state of mixed concentration and relaxation which so often eludes me; I either consciously tell myself to notice this and appreciate that, or I let go and float happily away into some list-making reverie or other in which my expensive ticket has bought me so much background music. What I would need, I know, to still my mind and open my ears, would be my knitting. I knit at home sometimes and listen to records, but it isn't the same. And once, in the summer, at an outdoor opera performance, where the sound was heavily miked to compete with passing ambulance sirens, overhead airplanes, and the general hustle and bustle of night in the park, where there was no place for purists, I looked over and saw that the woman on the next blanket was knitting, and felt a powerful sense of kinship and a fierce regret: this would have been my chance!

I dream of knitting at my children's sporting events. Sure, I would put down the sweater and cheer when my son came up to bat—but the league is scrupulously fair and rotates all the players in and out, and eight-year-old baseball can be a slow slow game, especially when the infield starts to crumble and every contact with the ball means another error and another base runner. On the other hand, I don't dream of taking my knitting to Fenway Park. There's too much standing up and sitting down, too many moments when a devoted Red Sox fan has to groan and cover her eyes, or clap her hands to accompany the traditional chant of "Yankees suck! Yankees suck!" (Sorry, that's the thing about being a Red Sox fan—doomed but loyal.) The knitting might easily fall to the floor of the stadium, and believe me, you don't want to know what's on the floor of the stadium, and you certainly don't want it clinging to your wool. (I do, however, sometimes knit at home while listening to particularly exciting games, but this belongs in another category, knitting to deal with stress and tension; we'll get to that soon enough.) But the little league games cry out for knitting, and so do all those Saturday soccer matches—and I just can't do it. Would it seem like too much of a stunt, would it seem that I was deliberately calling attention to the seriousness with which some parents take these sports? (The girls soccer league in which my daughter used to play was reduced to legislating certain games as "quiet-parent games," no yelling or cheering or instructing from the sidelines allowed—clearly, everyone should have been knitting.) Would it just seem, well, snotty? I guess I'm afraid it would, or else afraid that I, as one of the less-involved parents—it's never me passing around the who's-bringing-snacks sign-up, or organizing the extra practice session, or taking up a collection for the coaches' thank-you gift—would be getting kind of ostentatious in my detachment.

Oh, but even more, I dream of knitting at open school nights, at assemblies, at all the events my children's schools can throw at me. Knitting through the detailed presentation of the third-grade math curriculum, or the tenth-grade health syllabus. Knitting through that combination of extreme boredom and clutch-at-my-heart fascination to which motherhood opens the door. Come to think of it, I would like to go back in time and knit through my own high school years, through the boredom and self-consciousness of my high school classes, in fact, through all the boredom and self-consciousness and uncertainty and anxiety and fake sophistication of my adolescence.

But I'm getting off the track here. I'm starting to sound like the key is knitting through the bad experiences, through the tensions or through the stupefyingly boring moments. And certainly knitting has its place at those moments, as anyone who has ever knitted through the boring tension (or the tense boredom) of a bad airport delay can attest. Knitting can even help you through the genuinely tragic moments—I have many hospital memories from my training, of bedside knitters, mothers and grandmothers resolutely clicking away as the hospital day wore into the hospital night, and the nurses checked the vital signs and administered the medications. So yes, by all means, knit through the bad moments; soothe yourself and sometimes someone else—the child in the hospital bed, the worried travelers around you.

Make something hopeful and constructive of the times that yield up bad memories, and, always, with the power of the knitter, just plain make something beautiful. But consider now the occasions which are by no means bad moments, the opportunities when life is fine, but could be that much richer, that much fuller, that much more, if only we could knit.

For me, as I said, there's classical music. I like to imagine a beautiful concert hall full of dedicated knitters working away in rapt appreciation (and probably in rhythm) as an orchestra surges into full symphonic sound. Here comes the brass, here come the strings, here comes the stitch marker and the pattern repeat. Adagio, andante, fortissimo. Or alternatively, I like to imagine a string quartet playing just for me, as I sit appreciating and carefully stranding my different colors—such fine fingering, how very appropriate.

Or consider, if you will, the formal group dinner. The sitting around waiting for your table to be served—the salad course, the wine, the main course, the dessert. The rubber chicken and those strange little slightly undercooked carrots decorating the plate. The anticipation of the speeches. The speeches themselves. Perfectly worthy events, often in celebration or recognition of someone or something well worth recognizing. But oh, lord, if only I could bring my knitting.

This was, I have to admit, a fairly idle fantasy of mine, a kind of vague I-wish-I-could-bring-my-knitting-to-the-dinner-table yen that I had known for years, especially in those knitting-obsessed moments when a project took over my life, up until I attended

88

my first big knitting conference, a Stitches conference in 2001. At the dinner, I did in fact bring my knitting, and so, of course, did everyone else. We knit as we waited for them to serve our table, we knit while we waited for them to clear and serve the next course, we knit during the speeches. I had never felt such a sense of fellowship, and I have never so wholeheartedly enjoyed a "group event" dinner.

And I have some other settings in mind. Am I the only person who has ever thought about how well knitting would go with religious services? Has anyone ever tried it? Am I in violation of any major commandments in even suggesting it? And how about commencements, where you have to watch those other 200—or 2000—children walk across the stage? But no, I'm not bringing my knitting to dinner when it's not a knitting convention. I know better than that. I don't want to be anyone's eccentric or anyone's pooh-pooher.

But what I'm saying is, those settings, those occasions, need a little something to make them perfect. A subtle spice, a shake of salt. Something to bring out the complexity of their flavors, something, to mix a metaphor, to burnish them and make them shine. And it's not just a metaphor, either; recently I ate in a fancy restaurant (oh, I tell you, mine is a glamorous life—cruises, fancy restaurants) where they did not put salt and pepper shakers on the tables, presumably to convey to us that the food was exquisitely balanced and flavored by the personal hand of the chef, and should not be crudely doctored by the philistines (and doctors!) who were eating it and paying for it. But I like salt, and hard as I tried to appreciate the subtle interplay of herbs in my food, I wanted salt. Something was missing. I had to flag down a waiter and repress the urge to apologize to him for even asking. But then, when he was out of sight, I put some salt on my food. And suddenly the tastes came together and the moment was right. And when I dream about forbidden knitting opportunities, I am acknowledging moments that need that one extra element to transcend the ordinary and offer a hint of knitter's bliss.

This was a fantasy that came true—an editor who offered to send me anywhere I'd wanted to go so I could write about the experience. I think he was perhaps expecting a medical request—a famous surgeon that I longed to watch in action, a revolutionary new scientific breakthrough. Instead, I asked to be sent to attend—and write about—a workshop that Kaffe Fassett was leading at the Monterey Bay Aquarium in California. And off I went, unable to believe my luck, saying to myself over and over, when I grow up, I want to be a knitting journalist! So this is what I think of as my first (and perhaps my only) work of knitting journalism—and I can only hope I get the chance to do many more, when I grow up if not before.

GLORIOUS YARN
The Los Angeles Times Magazine, October 25, 1992

Right before Kaffe Fassett came to the United States to do a series of knitting workshops and promote his new book, he was asked to a dinner in London given by the American ambassador. The ambassador had invited the Queen of England, and to meet her he assembled 20 Americans, all living in Britain, all distinguished in their different fields. An author, a ballerina, an admiral, a Rhodes scholar—the British papers immediately began referring to them as the "American Top 20." Kaffe Fassett, who grew up in Big Sur, California, and has been living in Britain since 1964, was among those chosen. When the queen asked him what he did, he told her, and, he recalls with pleasure, she said immediately, "Oh, knitting; even I can do that!" Yes, says Fassett, that's exactly the point. "What I love about knitting is that it's humble and practical," he says. "It's just making a sweater or a sock. You're not only making a handsome and colorful object, but the process is a soothing, life-enhancing activity."

The objects that Kaffe (rhymes with safe) Fassett designs and knits are more than handsome and colorful. They are works of art, revolutionary works of craft, many-colored masterpieces that break all the sacred rules of handknitting—and they are, he insists, well within the reach of your average, everyday home knitter. He makes his theory a reality by leading workshops for average, everyday home knitters. Like me.

I can remember buying Fassett's *Glorious Knits* not long after it came out in 1985. I was browsing in the yarn store, turning over one pattern or another, looking for patterns suitable for beginners, for those marked "very easy." Then I saw this hardcover book, and on the cover was a woman wearing a stupendous yellow sweater. It was big and loose and draped comfortably over her body, and it seemed to be made out of 15 or 20 shades of yellow and gold and brown, patterned with large geometric stars in blue and gray. I flipped through the book. I had never seen anything like these designs; my very limited knitting life had included a couple of laboriously constructed sweaters knitted during my pregnancy, along with some booties that had turned out to be just as useless as all the other booties ever knitted. I had made my share of scarves, and, of course, I had, in a plastic bag in my bedroom, the obligatory Unfinished Sweater, left over from high school, a rather nice blue.

But I had never seen anything like these designs. Each pattern was based around a geometric motif—large steps, small steps, ikat stripe, outlined star, floating circles—and all of them knitted with what looked like hundreds of different colors. I had never seen anything so beautiful, and that is almost not hyperbole. I looked at the introduction: "Like many other crafts, knitting has the potential to create magic in our lives," it began. Whoever was writing, I believed him. I stared down at the photograph of the author in his studio: He sat barefoot on a stool in front of an enormous tapestry of Chinese vases. Next to him was a table, and piled under the table were neatly folded sweaters, glowing with those colors, dancing with those patterns, and above the picture were the words, "If knitting with colors turns out to be your particular road to self-expression, then you will have started on a marvelously rewarding and adventurous journey."

And so I bought the book—a hardcover book of obviously complicated knitting patterns, patterns I doubted I would ever be able to make. I was a medical student and not particularly wealthy; buying any hardcover book new was an unusual self-indulgence. I felt like a fool. But I knew that I had to own this book, had to get these pictures home and look at them one by one.

I was not alone. *Glorious Knits* sold more than 350,000 copies worldwide, a remarkable track record for a knitting book. I read the story of Fassett's life: brought up in Big Sur, he chose the name Kaffe from a children's book, trained as a painter, moved to London in the early '60s, discovered wools on a trip to a mill in Scotland, bought 20 colors, learned to knit on the train ride back and used all 20 colors in his very first sweater.

And now, with a mild sense of embarrassment, for the very first time in my life, I find myself writing an it-changed-my-life sentence. I have never gotten religion. I am deeply suspicious of all things New Age, and you will never catch me coming back from a workshop to announce that I have found my "inner child" or mastered the art of shaman drumming. But Kaffe Fassett's knitting designs changed my life. Look for colorways, he wrote, systems of color and shade that work together. Look at the world around you, at the colors that exist together in nature—and above all, look at the way colors work in decorative objects, in tapestries and porcelains and mosaics. It changed the way I looked at knitting; it changed the way I looked at the world.

I became someone who bought up single skeins of every color yarn that took my fancy, bringing them home against some large multicolor project I would someday do. Then, little by little, I began to do those projects. A scarf or two, a few easy striped sweaters for my son, then one for myself. As I advanced from medical student to pediatrician, I also advanced from timid, aspiring, sometime knitter, scared of patterns, to fanatic knitter-in-residence, with a bag of multicolor yarn. Knitting helped me get through my residency, kept me awake at conferences, comforted me when the world of the hospital seemed particularly unforgiving, particularly sad or scary. Sleep-deprived and distracted, I had no concentration to spare for perfect, classic knotless garments. I mixed colors and changed patterns around, and it worked. On some very fundamental level, I had been liberated.

So this is why it was a big deal for me to be sitting in Monterey, about to begin a several-day workshop on knitting with color with Fassett, who was traveling on a tour connected to the publication of his newest book, *Glorious Inspirations.* I was nervous and thrilled and also somewhat apprehensive. He would see me knit, and I have no talent at all in the visual arts; I would see him knit, and what if he turned out to be overly slick or just not very nice? What if I went home, and all his patterns had lost their magic?

DAY 1. I am one of the last to arrive at the Monterey Bay Aquarium, and our little group is led upstairs to the meeting room. The center of the room is occupied by thousands of balls of yarn, arranged in a kind of color wheel. A lake of yarn, a field of yarn, a thing of beauty all by itself. There are a number of women sitting in chairs around the yarn, talking quietly, drinking coffee and juice. And over on the side are Fassett and his assistant, Brandon Mably, the two of them needlepointing away for all they are worth on a long strip done in oranges and browns. Fassett is 54, with dark hair and remarkable light eyes; he himself, the master of color, when later asked to describe them, can do no better than "light gray blue."

With minimal introduction, they start the class by marching us back out of the room, on an expedition around the aquarium. Brandon Mably, energetic and resplendent in an ornate knitted waistcoat paired with a sequined baseball cap, serves as a kind of point man, or maybe bird dog; he scouts the exhibits ahead for particularly fascinating collections of color. He hurries back to report that we absolutely must look at one particular bit of reef, and we crowd around the tank. Fassett points out to us the magenta hue of a sea cucumber's foot next to its orange, tentacled head—"the Phyllis Diller hairdo." We move as a determined group through the aquarium sightseers, the families with strollers and children on class trips; they are all looking at fish, reading labels and identifying organisms, but we are looking only for color.

Back in our conference room, we watch a slide show, starting with pictures of Big Sur and Wales, Mably's home. "I worked from those grays," Fassett says, showing us a picture of Mably in a stone quarry. On to more designs, some of them breathtaking: the Roman glass shawl, with hundreds of tiny circles on a muted, variegated background, the "foolish-virgin" jacket with strong folk-art figures. And also pictures of the colors and the objects that inspire them: the reds of a Chelsea flower show, the Red Fort in India. Plugs for Fassett's knitting kits; this is available, that is available. And some statements of knitting philosophy: "When you run out of yarn is when the fun begins," Fassett tells us. "It's a very organic and exciting way of knitting." He speaks with British intonations, and though he is obviously strongly connected to the designs he is showing us, he is also obviously giving a talk he has given many times before. As a group, the students seem impressed but a little intimidated.

And now to the real business of the workshop. Each of us chooses a card to work from, a picture of a painting. A Matisse odalisque, a Klee composition, bold flowers on a black background, an Indian miniature. I end up with a Monet painting, purples and greens lower down opening up to tans and golds of sky, with tall, skinny poplar trees. We are instructed to paint with yarn; we are not trying to reproduce our cards, but we are working from their colors, each producing a piece of knitting inspired by a painting, reflecting the palette of the painting. And using a minimum of 20 colors, Fassett says, more if possible. Use 30 or 40. So we kneel among the yarns, trying to match colors out of the cards. We take our yarns back to our seats. We cast on.

I had promised my fellow knitters in Cambridge that I would ask Fassett what he really does with all the little dangling ends. I tend to leave these hanging, then go back over the finished garment with a crochet hook and twist them in. This is a tedious, not to say maddening, task. Fassett, in his books, speaks of working the ends in as he goes. And now he proposes to show us how, so we leave our chairs and gather around him, watching his fingers as he knits.

It is like watching an artist whose work has always meant an enormous amount to you paint a brand new, never-before-seen painting. But that's not all. It's the way his fingers dance. Yes, they are using many colors, and yes, they are neatly tucking the ends in as he goes, knitting American-style, yarn held in his right hand, pulling up the color he needs for each stitch. Sure and quick and much more complicated than ordinary knitting. He sits next to the big window that looks out over the bay, working out a new knitting pattern, lime green and tangerine trellises climbing up a background of richer, deeper colors. He is making up the pattern as he goes along, telling us he will later give it to one of his assistants, who will sort out the stitches and chart the colors for someone else to follow. The pattern grows under his hands, and his fingers dance.

Many of Fassett's inspirations come from the world of decorative arts. His newest book, *Glorious Inspirations,* is a collection of sources, objects to inspire needlework or knitting. Japanese fish tattoos, porcelain boxes sculpted to look like fruits, inlaid Italian wooden tabletops. He encourages the re-translation of the colors and patterns that talented eyes have drawn from nature and encourages the connection to traditional images and designs, even while changing the colors, the backgrounds, the rules. "I don't want to get wingding modern. I want it to have that grounded familiarity you get with old traditions, handsome simple motifs that we've loved in icons and Persian carpets," he says.

The double layering of one craftsman taking inspiration from another's interpretation of the world adds texture and complexity to the process of design as well as to the knitting itself. Fassett's readers and students are encouraged to join the chain of decorative arts, adapting someone else's adaptation, giving it a new form and, of course, a new function, making a soup dish into a sweater, a mosaic into a pillow. "When I painted, I always wanted to see my paintings in the environment of the world. You can put all the complexity of paintings and richness of color into a garment," Fassett says.

It's a consuming passion. Fassett has, he says, no social life. "I'm a total workaholic." In his studio in London, he employs several knitters, working on his original designs and on the special garments commissioned by the rich and famous. And then there are the convicts. Fassett and Mably have worked with murderers at the notorious British prison Wormwood Scrubs, where inmates are allowed to do needlework in their cells. The murderers, Fassett says, are "timid" about knitting and more likely to start with needlepoint; they go in for "quite exciting color." There was one prisoner who did knit, and enthusiastically: "I asked what he was in for, and it turned out he

was a thief; he used to steal Missoni sweaters. So he knew the value of knitting."
We are back in our seats now, our chosen yarns piled around us, knitting without
patterns, knitting with all those colors. What we are doing feels downright weird
and wrong to some women, striking off into the unpatterned unknown. Fassett
keeps encouraging us: We should do a little, then hang our work up on the wall with
pins and step back to look with him at where we're going. Most people seem to feel
shy about doing this. Finally one woman hangs up a narrow strip of knitting, steps
away from it and complains that she can't see all the different colors she has carefully
used in her piece. "Yes," Fassett says, looking with her from across the room, "you
worked very hard for that dark smudge." We all laugh, and then he is much gentler,
encouraging this knitter, telling her to look at her card, to stop focusing on the darker
end of the spectrum, to try for "luminous—get more luminous." He is in the center
picking out some colors for her to add in, down on his knees snatching up balls
of yarn.

As we sit and knit, even without patterns, we are relaxing; we are, all of us, people
who are happy knitting. Sitting in a big circle around the yarn, knitting and listening
to the water noises from the bay outside the window, we introduce ourselves, moving
around the circle. "I've been knitting for years, and I love it. It's what I do instead
of collecting knickknacks, I buy yarn. The two spare bedrooms in my house are for
yarn," says Penny Boone, from Torrance. Ann Hodge is a retired elementary-school
principal from Niagara Falls; when she travels, she says, she likes to go looking for
interesting yarns. Says Lorraine Perry, a science teacher in San Francisco: "For me,
there's always been a conflict between arts and sciences—a knitting conference at
the aquarium is perfect!" Kathleen Dowell from Fresno describes herself: "I do dental
hygiene to support my knitting habit." Norma Westwick from Sacramento confesses:
"When we went to Europe, I bought yarn in every country. My ex-husband didn't like
me knitting while we were watching TV, so I gave it up for a while."

"The knitting or the TV?" someone asks.

"The husband!" she answers, to general applause.

97

Our knitted swatches are growing. People are unwilling to break for lunch, hanging on for one more row, a few more colors. I look at the swatches around me, and a number seem to me supremely organized, falling into natural patterns created by people with excellent visual instincts. My own is fairly chaotic: lots of colors flickering in and out. If I hold my head on one side and squint to blur my vision, I guess it looks a little bit Impressionistic.

After lunch, we knit the afternoon away. Fassett is still needlepointing long strips, putting his work down to comment whenever someone pins her swatch on the wall, something we are all still quite reluctant to do. He urges us to come forward, urges us also to relax and talk a little more. He even suggests that we might sing. Some workshop groups do. But we are not so cheerfully spontaneous.

My swatch, like those of the others, is beginning to trail a large rat's nest of yarn; every time I add in a new color and use it for a couple of stitches, I leave the rest to drag along, thinking maybe I'll want some more a few rows down the line—but by a few rows down the line, I have been seduced by some new, paler purple, some flesh-pink chenille.

By the end of the afternoon, many of us are confused. Are we making messes, or are we painting with yarn? It still feels peculiar and irregular to be out here, now well into these knitted squares, making things up as we go along. "I took my mother to one of these classes," Fassett says cheerfully. "Afterward, she didn't knit for two years!"

"This is so easy—why did I wait so long?" asks one of the women. I actually feel silly that I needed someone to come along and tell me that I didn't have to follow all the rules. And I wonder: Did Fassett see his way around conventional knitting because he is a man, and therefore by definition unconventional as a knitter? There are, after all, no men in this workshop; Fassett and Mably refer to their students as "our ladies."

"When I first started to knit," says Fassett, "I used to think, 'This is something that could put the world to rights.' I know that creativity is my salvation and my sanity; I can't help feeling it would be a tremendous boon to other neurotic, frustrated people."

DAY 2. People have loosened up a little. One woman says she had a vision last night and now knows exactly where she is going with her knitting. Another announces that she decided to disregard the rule Fassett made yesterday about no ripping out. She went ahead and ripped out some bad stuff, she says happily; after all, isn't Fassett the one who tells us to break rules? I have also had a vision in my little way; the night before, I had imagined the randomness of my piece resolving into solid vertical patterns. So I pick six colors and find my way out of a somewhat confused patch of blue sky (with a couple of different blues and even a purple mixed up in it) into five broad stripes, climbing up.

Mably is traveling around the circle, both he and Fassett insisting that we have to be braver about pinning our work on the wall and stepping back to regard it. We need that perspective to see what colors are called for, where we should go next. But we are all still painfully shy. Fassett and Mably warn us that the day will end with a "crit," for which all the knitting will be displayed, with Fassett discussing what each of us has done.

Mably insists that I hang up my swatch; he and Fassett stare at it. I need to break up those vertical blocks, speckle them with pink and green, Fassett says. This is how his designs become more and more baroque; spotted stripes, checkered borders. I add a single strip of green. Other swatches go up on the board, some very lovely indeed. Fassett himself seems more involved and interested than yesterday; with real knitting projects to comment on, he is lively and excited. He seems to care about each and every swatch; the colors speak to him, and he answers. And he seems to be looking forward to the crit.

Lunch. More knitting. More knitting talk. People down on their knees among the yarn, looking for that one last color. And then, finally, the crit. All of our swatches are pinned up on the wall, each next to the card that supposedly inspired it. Fassett takes his position beside this wall of knitted squares and colored cards. And here is the most remarkable surprise: The wall is beautiful. Each swatch is clearly related to one of the pictures, and the pictures do not necessarily go together in any way, but what we have made is a patchwork of color and the reflection of color that is truly, to use Fassett's word, glorious. I cannot believe that we have done this, created this group work of art, or that my own square of would-be-Monet purples and golds and blues and greens is really glowing up there on the wall, a luminous patch of water-flower colors and sky.

Fassett goes through each swatch, looking to see how the colors from the card are used, how the piece works as knitting. His highest praise is to tell someone, "This could be a sweater." But he has something kind to say to everyone: "This is very emotional color, but that little scrap of turquoise is the jewel of the piece…that peach is wonderful with the gold; that swatch I could see turning into a jumper (pullover)… this one finally deals with the greens in that card, very good…" He points to mine, and I am suddenly tense. "Look down here at the beginning, very tight with dark shadows; did it come up to the light! There's a wonderful underwater sunlit quality."

And now, at the end, people are photographing each other next to the wall of swatches. It's time to drive down to Big Sur for dinner at Fassett's family's restaurant, Nepenthe. Mably is gathering up the yarn, sorting and packing it. Surreptitiously, I am taking more bits and pieces of the colors in my swatch. Who knows, I might do more of it someday. But what I am really imagining is a wall in my house covered with 10 or more of these color experiments. What a thing to do when your life needs color and creativity: Pick a painting, match the colors, knit a swatch. Paint with wools.

It's true, I still think, that I have no particular talent for the visual arts; all around me are people with better senses of pattern, surer hands with color. But even so, there is a distinct messianic fervor behind the workshop, behind the books, behind the man. "Half my creativity is from my own personal statement," Fassett says. "The other half is dragging the world along on my trip."

Knitting is a journey. Knitting is a passion. Knitting is a craft. Knitting is an addiction. When I write for a knitting magazine, I don't generally find myself trying to explain why I knit, because I assume that each reader already understands on some deep true level—that's why we're here, me writing and you reading, both of us eager to get back to our own knitting. So it's really more in articles for non-knitting publications (as we might call all newspapers and most magazines) that I find myself trying to explain what knitting means in my life and why it matters. Here is an essay about what happens when I stop knitting, and what it means.

A PASSION FOR PURLS
Victoria Magazine, January 2002

There are various indicators that I use to let me know when my life is veering somehow off course, when everything is leaning towards the out of whack. When I stop reading books I haven't read before, for example, and retreat exclusively into the familiar comfort of the books I already know and love. Or when I realize I haven't gone grocery shopping in a couple of weeks, and have been feeding my family on takeout and restaurant stops. These are warnings that the balance has shifted, that life is too stressed, or my mind too roiled to take care of what needs to be taken care of. These activities are, if you will, the canaries in the mine shaft; as long as there's air enough to permit shopping and cooking and reading new novels, there's air enough to breathe.

But my truest and most reliable indicator is knitting. Every year it happens once or twice: I find myself in the middle of some stressed-out complicated day, I close my eyes and try to promise myself a little treat of one kind or another, and I realize, always with a certain shock, *hey, I'm not knitting anything these days!* Maybe life has just become too complicated—too many things due, too much time committed. Or maybe I'm emotionally off course—too anxious, too down in the dumps, too wired. Or maybe my most recent knitting project has come up against some problem—it's not turning out to be the right size, or I've arrived at directions I don't quite understand, or I've discovered a bad mistake many many rows back, and have to make the agonizing decision to rip out precious inches of my own hard work. Or maybe—and most likely—it's some unfortunate combination of all these things; a complex period in my life, a difficult emotional moment, an unfortunate snag (perhaps literally) in the current project.

But the result of this concatenation of circumstances is this: I stop knitting. I don't consciously give it up, of course, or put it aside—I just let it go, the way it's so easy to let something go when life gets complicated. And then I stumble along until I hit my moment of epiphany, that reliable instance of insight when the lights go on and I can suddenly see and understand my own empty hands.

When I am knitting, I am OK. When I have a project going—really going, I mean, not stalled on some agonizing indecision about to rip or not to rip—it gradually reaches out to take over my life. I drive my car from place to place, fantasizing about how the meeting will begin and I will reach for my needles, about new colors to join and interesting pattern complexities waiting up ahead. I move through my days—practice medicine, care for my family, attend to all the paperwork and phone calls and email messages and beeper pages which are the stuff of modern life, attend meetings, give talks—and all the time, there is a colored background in my mind, the stripes of the sweater, the fruit pattern of the mittens, the color complexities of the blanket. When I am knitting, I am OK.

I have been knitting on and off for more than thirty years—but note, please, the on and off. My grandmother taught me, and I made a scarf or two. I fussed with scarves and sweaters in high school, flirted for the first time with circular needles in college, and finally became a true and total addict in medical school, buying the first few balls of what is now an enormous stash, and discovering the vicarious joys of reading knitting books and knitting magazines. I have outfitted children—my own three and miscellaneous others—in sweaters and mittens, experimented with the geometrics of the triangular shawl, which grows from one single starting stitch, welcomed new babies with hats and blankets, and even danced one quick tango with lace knitting, making myself a patterned shawl in matching green cotton and chenille. I have what knitters have—a crowded shelf of pattern books, enormous plastic tubs stuffed full of odd balls of yarn, and a thousand projects in mind to do someday, when the time is right. And yet I can easily and instantly be seduced away from all these plans by the right yarn, the right suggestion, the right moment: socks! Cool! I've never made socks—it's time to make socks—out of the way, everybody, it's sock woman!

What does it bring to my life? Why do I love it so, why do I need it so? I know that when I am knitting I am OK, and that when I am not knitting, I am probably not quite so OK. In fact, I can pinpoint some of the reasons that from time to time my hands go slack and I lose the knitting, and I can see quite clearly that one of my first certain steps back towards balance involves reaching for those needles again. But why—what do I pick up along with the stitches?

As any knitter will tell you, this is more than a hobby. There's an addiction of the mind, an addiction of the spirit, and even an addiction of the fingers. Mental knitting goes on all the time—I deconstruct garments that I see on other people, or that I see in pictures, and I put them back together. I stare at boring lecturers and across their faces I see stretched a newly knitted swatch, growing in color and complexity and texture. And my fingers definitely crave the repetition and the rhythm, the tension of the yarn which keeps them tied to one another—when I read knitting instructions, my fingers move.

But let's talk about the spiritual addiction. OK, I don't knit to provide my family with cheaper sweaters—we all know that this is no way to save money—and that any guess at the cost of these garments would have to factor in hours and hours of my priceless time. And I don't knit to prove my own feminine skills, nor even to avoid the dangers of idle hands. I'm too far gone for any of that—neither thrifty nor particularly skilled in the womanly arts, nor even desperately eager to be thought so. So what is it—what do I get from all this knitting, and what is missing when I take a hard look at myself and don't see any yarn or needles?

What is missing, I think, is a special sense of portable everyday serenity. Knitting brings something into my life that I might also get—but generally don't—from great music, religion, or the contemplation of majestic natural beauty. When I knit, my soul is calmed, and, sometimes, exalted. But it's an every-day exaltation, a calm domestic serenity, easily transported from place to place in a cloth bag—and that is, I suspect, what makes it traditional women's work, a source of serenity involving no heroics, no great outlay on equipment, and carefully tied to all that is most useful and most motherly.

Knitting for me is meditation and mantra both; my mind repeats and reiterates the instructions of the rhythm: knit one purl one, even as my fingers carry out the instructions, and I rejoice quietly in the close connection between injunction and product. I feel the yarn slip along round my finger, advancing with each stitch, and I finger the growing piece of knitted goods. And truly, there are moments now and then when it seems to me that I can also smell the comforting warmth of the wool, perhaps even taste it (you aren't supposed to bite yarn, you're supposed to cut it neatly—but perhaps I can admit to that small sin)—when all my senses are completely caught up.

The great boon of knitting in my life, of course, is that even while that kind of sensory involvement is going on, I can still be paying attention to something else. I am a confirmed knitter-in-meetings, knitter-in-lectures, knitter-in-the-car (passenger side only—that's my car with the SAVE A LIFE—DON'T KNIT AND DRIVE bumper sticker on it). I can listen to important information or make cheerful conversation or even look regularly out the window, and keep on knitting. Needless to say, this limits the complexity of the patterns I take on (and needless to say, if the meeting is very long, or the lecture very dull, or the landscape unappealing, I may find myself slipping into that trance-like state where I AM my knitting, and my mind has no room for anything else). And I know that people sometimes look at me dubiously—the medical world is not necessarily friendly to knitters. I, of course, always feel that lecturers should be glad to see that I have brought my knitting—when I have to give a talk, I look out at the knitters in the audience and know that there are at least a few people sitting there positively looking forward to the hour to come. Without my knitting, stuck at a medical lecture, what am I? Just another fidgety listener, easily diverted into making lists of important things to do as soon as they let me out of here.

Knitting for me is serenity and comfort, a steady rhythm that underlies the rest of daily life like a heartbeat. Knitting is also, I have come to realize, my chance in life to work with color and texture and design. As a writer, I work with words, and gladly. I love the sound of words, the sight of words on the page—I am easily intoxicated by words, amused by words, rocked and shocked by words. As a physician, I do my best to read and understand the hidden codes of the human body, its aches and agonies, its growth and health. But as a knitter, I reach for subtly varying shades of red and brown, or for a great heap of gentle gray; as a knitter I play with stripes and checks and flowers, with color on color and pattern on pattern. There is nowhere else in my life where things can be arranged and rearranged until a taste for visual harmony is satisfied. Certainly not in my home, which looks like the home of a family with three children and low domestic standards. Certainly not at work—what kind of doctor would I be if I held up the process of diagnosis or discussion to strive for niceties of color and shade? Knitting is my chance to—oh, well, let's go ahead and say it—to create, with color. To make something which wasn't there before, and to make it beautiful. And I have come to understand that I need that in my life, that chance to work with color and texture and form, to create not with words, but with yarn. I need it, I want it, I love it. And when things go wrong and I put the knitting down, something is missing, and I know it. And I know, as I acknowledge what's missing, what my next step has to be: chase down a stalled project, leaf through a knitting magazine. Reach for the yarn, reach for the needles, reach for the rhythm, reach for the colors. Without it, life is colder and duller and my hands are still.

Sometimes I think that every sweater has its story. The life details of the knitter, the emotions of the moment, the relationship of the knitter to the person who will wear the sweater (which may mean her relationship to herself), the anticipation of starting, the actual circumstances of the knitting, the emotion of watching it grow.... A good story-teller could get the story of a life—or a piece of a life story—from a close analysis of the making and wearing of any handknit sweater. And then there are the stories that don't tie up neatly into conventional endings, like my son's star sweater...

THE GREAT UNFINISHABLE
KnitLit Too, 2004

I am not talking about your everyday run-of-the-mill unfinished knitting project here. I have plenty of those—don't we all? I have a pair of gorgeous, if rather oversized, socks, all done up to the kitchener stitch joining the toes—and there was something incomprehensible about those particular instructions, and I put the socks down, meaning to figure out how to join the toes from some other set of instructions—and I just never did. But I will some day. Or there's that elaborate intarsia cardigan I have been knitting for myself for a good ten years—the diagram is kind of hard to follow, and I somehow ran out of interest in the pattern, and every winter I pick it up and add a couple of inches, and I really do believe that eventually it will just finish growing and be done (I mean, I remember when it was just a back, now everything's done except a sleeve and a bit) although, again, it might take me a couple of years to get up the energy for blocking and finishing and decorating. No, my bins are full of projects that I truly believe I'm going back to when the time is right, just as they're full of patterns I'm going to follow before I die and even plastic bags of wool bought with some very particular fantasy in mind. But even those unstarted projects don't seem as distant and unreachable as my Great Unfinishable, and I have come to wonder whether every serious knitter, over the years, at some point accumulates a project which is clearly meant to remain ethereally, aspiringly, only partially done. Mine is a sweater that I started making for my oldest child when he was two, and I was an intern doing my training in pediatrics. I made it big, deliberately, as I always do when knitting for kids, both because I think loose clothing is always the way to go with children, and because I want to leave myself a little slack in terms of timing. So I aimed for a sweater that would be very big on a two-year-old, look fine on a four-year-old, and maybe even live on into kindergarten. That child, who is nineteen, has just finished his first year of college, and he has done it without the sweater.

It was easily the most ambitious project I had attempted. It was a Kaffe Fassett design, row on row of outlined stars, and I assembled several dozen yarns in each color category—the centers of the stars, the outlines, the background. I worked with lengths of yarn and makeshift bobbins dangling in all directions and a tattered photocopy of the pattern. I made the whole front of the sweater and it was beautiful. My son admired it too—he knew it was his star sweater, and he liked me to hold it up against his sturdy little chest to see how far I had gotten.

The problem was—well, the problem could have been so many things. I needed to knit in meetings and seminars, and this sweater, with its constant bobbin-tending and its ostentatious multicolored complexity, was obviously wrong. Even if I had absorbed the geometric pattern completely and didn't need to check the instructions, even if I knew that I was listening to every word that was said, it still looked to everyone else in the room like my concentration had to be all on that intricate elaborate sweater. It called for comment and admiration, and what I needed was something simple and unobtrusive. And the truth is, even though I had absorbed the geometric pattern, that sweater was pretty busy and my eyes and brain did tend to get caught up in the knitting. *Which color next to which, how many rows to go in the star, how many rows of stars to go in the front, can you believe how beautiful this is, can you believe I am creating such a thing?* And then, on top of that, I stopped feeling comfortable bringing the sweater out of the house with me at all—so many hours of work, so many decisions, so many damn bobbins—what if it were lost or stolen? What if one of my colleagues got pizza on it at the next noon conference?

It did occur to me that all of these same considerations would apply to the sweater itself, if I finished it and put it on my child. But I don't really think that any of this was rational. Nothing was going to happen to the sweater at work. If I had completed it, I would have put it on my son and it would have withstood the various spills and scrimmages of childhood. No: I think that what happened to me with that sweater was that I came up against my Great Unfinishable, the project which, for complex reasons involving my temperament, the shape of my life, my beliefs, and my destiny, was always meant to remain in progress.

I think about that story—I don't know whether it's true, but it's certainly told often enough—that master Oriental rug makers always deliberately include one mistake because nothing made by human hands is supposed to be absolutely flawless. I wonder if in the life of a knitter—or of certain knitters—there needs to be a project that will always exist as something attempted but not fully attained, a thing of beauty that is not yet a thing of use. All I can tell you is that, unlike those untoed socks, which periodically nag at me, I seem to be at peace with the star sweater in its partial state. I think it's beautiful, and I pull it out and look it over every now and then and marvel at it, but I don't think seriously that it's getting to be time to pick it up again.

Sometimes an unfinished project signals something wrong, something pathological, something stifled in a life; consider the would-be writer who struggles with a never-to-be-finished novel which somehow blocks all other possible projects. And some famous unfinished artistic projects were overtaken by death or fate or history. Consider Leonardo's bronze horse, which he had to abandon in 1499 when the French attacked Milan; the Italians used the bronze to make weapons, and the French, after taking over the city, destroyed the clay model by using it for target practice. But there are also plenty of famous Leonardo projects that were left unfinished by the artist—drawings for paintings he never painted, paintings he started but didn't complete. We tend to see those as evidence of his fervent teeming creativity (not that I'm suggesting any comparisons to me and my star sweater!).

Many of us, I think, without holding claims to renaissance genius, live happily with a never-to-be-finished something. You can be a busy and productive writer who treasures somewhere in a folder a partial manuscript, an attempt at putting down some inspiration which transported you and lifted you—but you didn't quite get all the way. I'm sure there are knitters out there who finish every single thing they start, but I bet there are a lot of us with lovely and beloved part-way projects.

The child for whom the star sweater was originally started now wears mostly teeshirts with in-joke slogans and jeans from the Gap. In fact, my youngest child is now, at eight, too big to wear the sweater. But somehow I don't feel like I missed my chance, or like I let something precious go to waste. Instead, I think that sweater supplied beauty and aspiration and mental exercise and a vast rainbow of color back at a time I needed it. I think that taking it on and learning to follow the instructions led me much further than I had ever been into the intricacies of complicated knitting. With every other project with ambitious colorwork that I have ever contemplated, a reassuring voice in my head has pointed out that next to the star sweater, this would be simple. I treasure what I actually created, and what I dreamed of creating; I treasure my own ambition, and my willingness to push against the limitations of my skill and the realities of my daily life.

But will I ever get to treasure that sweater, complete in all its glory? Ever get to see it worn by some important child or other? Some far off unimaginable niece or nephew or, dare I even say it, grandchild? To be honest, right now I don't think in terms of relearning that geometric pattern and sorting out those bobbins and dangling ends; I have a long and at times onerous "to do" list where knitting projects are concerned, and I regularly ignore it and buy new yarn for some new scintillating darling that has caught my eye. The star sweater is nowhere on my list at all.

But maybe one of the joys of a Great Unfinishable is the distant tantalizing possibility that I will change, or that life will change. I do keep the half-made sweater in a bag together with all the different balls of yarn. I know where the pattern is—in the Kaffe Fassett book on my shelf. Perhaps some day I will be a different knitter, a different person, a woman who might actually finish that sweater. Perhaps I will surprise myself—and the chance to do just that is part of what I treasure in that plastic bag full of many many different colored yarns and some rows of geometric stars.

And so, after many essays in which I wrote as the knitting doctor, I finally got to be the knitting patient. I fell in the line of duty—injured my hand by knitting and needed to get it repaired so I could go on knitting.

HAND SURGERY
Knitter's Magazine, Spring 2003

"It's a repetitive stress injury," I told the hand surgeon, as he examined my right hand. "I'm absolutely sure it's from knitting."

Not only from knitting, but to tell the truth, I was sure I knew the knitting project and the needles responsible. I was making scarves out of beautiful ribbon-flecked variegated yarn that knitted up into a fabric that looked like it was dotted with sequins. I had a circular size 13 needle to knit with back and forth, and I was just plain intoxicated by watching the scarves grow under my fingers with those big stitches. They were, among other joys, absolutely perfect car projects; I didn't have to look closely to knit, and every time I did look down, I could rejoice in the visibly lengthening material in my hands. So last summer when I spent a couple of days on a driving trip through Wyoming with a friend, I seized the opportunity and I seized that circular needle.

And I just plain didn't stop. Ready, set, go, and sometimes you just keep on going. You know those addictive episodes, when you knit past fatigued fingers, or past weariness and bedtime, those slightly zen times when you become one with your knitting? Mind you, I don't know how much honor there is in becoming one with a garter stitch scarf; some dazzling intricate pattern taking shape under my fingers would make a better story. But there I was and there was the scarf, and I couldn't stop. I finished a blue-and-sea green scarf and immediately cast on for a red-and-purple scarf. Outside the window of the car, Wyoming moved past, deserts and mountains, cattle grazing in the vast stretches of empty land.

Now, I could tell by the time I had been knitting for a couple of hours that there was a slightly tender spot on my right palm. I knit continental style, so my right needle basically does all the work, and as I manipulated this particular short metallic needle, joined to its twin by a thick clear cable, I was aware that the needle's end, the place where hard metal met soft plastic, was pressing repeatedly against this one sore spot, about half an inch below the base of my pinky. It wasn't really painful, just slightly tender, as I said, and I rather liked the idea that I might be developing a knitting callous. Mostly, though, I just wanted to keep knitting. Maybe exercise addicts experience this same drive—ready, set, go, and sometimes you just don't want to stop, even if it hurts.

And on we rolled across Wyoming, along the southernmost of the three passes through the Big Horn Mountains, south to the desert hot springs town of Thermopolis, where we soaked in a mineral pool with some passing Hell's Angels (never mind, it's another story) and then south again to Laramie and on to Denver. My friend basically did all the driving. "I like to drive, and I never get to drive long distances," she said. "OK," I said. "I like to knit."

The spot on my palm never got very sore at all. But it didn't go on to develop into a callous, either. Instead, about a month later, I realized that there was a new and alien lump on my hand, a hard round ball the size of a small green pea. It felt a little bit tender and a little bit—well, funny. I didn't like having it touched or pressed. I changed the position of my hands on the steering wheel when I drove. I didn't even want to think about using that size 13 knitting needle again. I noticed it when I was typing, when I was knitting with any needle at all, when I was chopping onions—whenever I used my hands.

And I hated it. I can be pretty tough about big serious pain, but I am a total self-pitying wimp when it comes to small, nagging discomforts. I had no doubt about what this thing on my hand was—it was a knitting injury, an artifact of repetitive stress and repetitive use—and I wanted it gone.

The hand surgeon told me it was probably a ganglion cyst—they're most common on the back of the wrist and the hand, and they tend to afflict people who do a lot of typing. They can get quite large—mine was small and insignificant by ganglion cyst standards—and they aren't dangerous. But I wanted it gone. The surgeon thought he might be able to break it up by sticking it with a hypodermic syringe, so he tried that, but the cyst was persistent (no pun intended). He told me that if I really wanted it gone, I would have to have surgery. I want it gone, I said. I can't drive comfortably, I can't type comfortably, and most of all, I can't knit comfortably.

"Oh, yes," he said. "You mentioned that you thought this might be connected to knitting." "It's a repetitive stress injury," I said. "It's from this number 13 circular needle."

I wasn't absolutely sure he was convinced, and I thought about explaining to him that my own medical student stint in surgery was heavily influenced by my experience in embroidery and knitting. I might not have known much anatomy (OK, I didn't know much anatomy), but I could set beautiful, even stitches along an incision, and I understood the idea of a "purse string" suture the very first time it was explained to me, and I wasn't bad at tying knots, either.… But I let it go. He was the doctor and I was the patient, and eventually the day came and I went in for day surgery to get rid of my ganglion cyst.

Now certainly, it's almost always salutary for a doctor to get a turn at being the patient, and here I had this ideal not-life-threatening, not-debilitating opportunity. And I have to say, it was kind of fascinating. It was day surgery, and I was wide awake—I could have had a sedative, but I didn't want one, since I just can't ever get over my alarm about people putting medications into my IV. I had IVs started in both my hands, and I was efficiently rolled into the operating room and shifted onto the operating table, prepped and draped, with my right arm extended out onto a special crosspiece and a drapery erected so I couldn't see what was happening beyond my right shoulder, much as I would have liked to—or at least, much as I thought I would have liked to.

113

Well, what they basically did was squeeze all the blood out of my right arm by wrapping it tightly, starting at the fingertips, in a giant rubber band. They kept on wrapping, right up to the elbow, then up my upper arm all the way to my armpit, and then they clapped on what felt like the world's largest, thickest tourniquet, to keep the blood from returning. At around this point it occurred to me that someone was about to mess around with my right hand—my knitting hand! The tourniquet felt monstrously tight; it was hard to believe my arm and my hand would survive this with anything like their former vigor and flexibility. I started worrying—perhaps you will think it was a little late to start worrying, but there it is—it had suddenly and forcefully occurred to me that life with a right hand that didn't work properly would be a very different life. I suppose that if I could draw or paint or play the piano, I would probably have thought of that all along. But I can't draw or paint or play the piano to save my life, and though I depend on my driving skills as much as any mother of three, and look on typing as my emotional lifeline, the thing that I was thinking, lying on that operating table, was, "What if I can't knit comfortably when this is over? What if something goes wrong and I can't knit any more?" And then, alternately, I thought about saying, "If you don't take this tourniquet off, I am going to scream!" But I kept quiet, and I thought about knitting.

Well, still and all, it was a very small ganglion cyst and a very small procedure. The surgeons excised it, and when they showed it to me, it looked even smaller than I had imagined, a little scrap of tissue, dropped into a bottle of preservative and sent off to be checked. They sewed me up and then, in a moment of transcendent beauty, they took off that damn tourniquet and my arm started to come back to life.

I recovered. I tried to keep my stitches dry, no easy task when infection control policies require that you wash your hands before and after touching every patient, and it's flu season to boot. Let's just say I wore a lot of plastic gloves and used up a lot of the band-aids we keep around for after shots. Two weeks later, the stitches came out, and I was delighted to have my hand back—no more cyst, no more sutures, nothing that shouldn't be there. I have a slightly pink oval on my hand now, nothing more, though it's a little bit more tender than the rest of my palm. I've tried knitting, using long straight needles, which do not press anywhere near there, and that was fine, though I was conscious of protecting the spot. I'm going to buy size 13 straights and finish that red-and-purple scarf. And yes, I do believe that I will play the piano again some day—I mean, that I will once again, someday soon, sit in the car and look out at the world passing by and knit without thinking of my hands and their complex anatomy. I will knit addictively and obsessively, though I promise that next time I get a sore spot, I really will stop. But after all, in a certain sense I am my repetitive stress injury—or repetitive strain injury—or repetitive use injury. Call it what you like, but I am my repetitive strain and stress, my repetitive use. Some of your medical story may be the story of things that come out of the blue and happen to you, but some of your medical story is about who you are and how you live. I had to have hand surgery because I knit too much. It makes a certain kind of sense. And next time I find myself grudging high insurance premiums and wondering whether I am subsidizing the injury-prone skiers, or the heavy smokers, I can remind myself that we all take certain risks, and that into each life, a certain amount of repetitive use must fall.

At some point, the first sentence of this essay began to sing itself inside my head. It wasn't necessarily an essay, it was just a sentence, as if I were sitting in a circle of strangers, playing some introductions game in which you got 10 words with which to sum yourself up. I had my ten words (well, eleven), my sentence, my explanation. It would pop into my head as I was falling asleep, and hang there like some profound spiritual message from the unseen world. But since I wasn't sitting in a circle of strangers, wasn't introducing myself in any circumstances where this line was appropriate, I finally wrote it down and tried to figure out what it meant. Knitting is a journey, a passion, a craft, an addiction—but knitting is also a way of observing my own life and times, my chaos and my good intentions, my talents and my limitations, my tastes and my compulsions. So allow me to introduce myself…

CONFESSIONS OF A TIGHT KNITTER
Knitter's Magazine, Fall 2004

I am a tight knitter who likes to wear loose clothing. These are two attributes I can claim without hesitation, two attributes which are somehow bound up into my voluntary preferences, my involuntary reactions, and my very nerve endings, two attributes which will never vary with the seasons.

A few weeks ago, I tried to take a personality test, a self-assessment which was meant to kick off a complete (and complex) evaluation process which would yield me some basic essential information about what kind of person I really am. Once I had completed this profile of myself, I was assured, I would end up with self-knowledge which would help me understand myself and my interactions with others; I would become more effective in the workplace and more understanding at home. I sat there looking at a list of adjectives, assigned to pick which ones applied to me and which ones didn't. The problem was, each adjective called forth a kind of dialogue. *Confident.* Am I confident? Well, sure, sometimes I'm confident. On my own ground,

I'm confident. When it comes to public speaking, I'm pretty confident. So sure, let's choose confident. But wait, think about what a wimp I was last week when the emergency room resident disagreed with my medical judgment—sometimes I'm not confident at all….and look how I'm wavering over choosing the words—would a confident person waver like this? So maybe I'm not confident—but then what about arrogant? I know I'm *arrogant* now and then—call it an occupational hazard of being a doctor—but can I be *arrogant* if I'm not *confident*?

OK, *anxious*. Well, certainly sometimes I'm very anxious. On the other hand, sometimes it's appropriate to be anxious. And I don't really think I'm anxious all the time—except sometimes I go through more anxious periods.

Never mind, how about *even-tempered*? I guess I'm even-tempered—except, of course, when I'm not. But how can you be unevenly even-tempered?

I went down the list, inclined to circle pretty much each word, but add some qualifiers: sometimes I'm this, occasionally I'm that, when I haven't slept well, I'm the other thing. And don't even ask what I am on a long family car trip when the kids are fighting in the back seat. What kind of person, I wondered, irritably, goes down a list like this and knows absolutely which words to circle? A *confident* person? An *arrogant* person? Am I, perhaps, in the end, just an *irritable* person?

So I'm not very good at these self-assessments. (I think I used to be better at those magazine quiz scenarios which used to turn up in *Cosmopolitan Magazine* when I was in college, and which I remember as group enterprises: four college girls lying around in a dormitory room reading the questions aloud: *Test yourself: are you a good friend. You've noticed your best friend's guy looking your way, and now he's called to ask whether you'd like to go out dancing while she's out of town. What's your reaction? A: You tell him to go take a long walk off a short pier: friends come first! B: Suggest making it a foursome when your gal-pal gets back.* And so on. I was pretty good at those, because you could always tell which choice would get you the most good-friend points, and I like to do well on tests.) I couldn't accumulate enough choices to qualify for my total personality profile, so I never did find out what kind of person I really am, and my interactions, at home and at work, have not improved. But it did get me thinking about what my real and essential attributes are, about which descriptors I could unequivocally accept as applying to me, describing me, defining me—not just at random moments but always and absolutely.

That's how I got to this: I am a tight knitter who likes to wear loose clothing. And although I don't think I'm going to go fulltime into the business of multiple-choice character analysis, I am wondering how much is included and implied in that description, how much psychology and personality, how much neurological hard-wiring and how much experience and personal development.

I have always been a tight knitter. My grandmother taught me to knit, and she knit continental style, so consequently I have never learned to "throw" the yarn. I control gauge and tension by keeping the yarn wrapped around my left index finger, and I tend to wrap it pretty tight. By the time I'm far enough into any project, the particular feel of that yarn around that finger has become part and parcel of whatever I'm knitting, a groove worn into the skin which communicates the ply and the softness and the stretchiness and the silkiness and the fuzziness of that particular material way down deep into my fingers, and maybe into my soul. I tend to make tight, even little stitches, and if one somehow comes out a little bit looser than the others, I am willing to pick my way painstakingly along the row and neaten things up, loop by loop, until the excess can be hidden over at the seam. I knit, I suppose you would have to say, like a miser, or maybe like a box-checker and a list-maker, or even a little bit of an obsessive-compulsive—certainly not like a free spirit, an artist, or an airy sprite. And the truth is, I am a list-maker and a box-checker, and I certainly have something of the obsessive in my makeup, and to me, all of those terms actually sound somewhat complimentary.

On the other hand, that isn't the whole real me either—so here I am back to circling the words on the personality inventory and deciding that I'm a little bit of everything, at least some of the time. No one who looked at the way I live, at my general randomness and my clutter and my chaos, could describe me as obsessively neat. My lists are full of boxes that never in fact get checked off—testaments to the great sense of accomplishment I get from drawing up the lists themselves. You wouldn't look at me, or at the way my family works, and conjure words like "schedule" and "order." In fact, if you wanted to be polite, you would probably take refuge in "bohemian" or "artistic," or even, god help us, call me a free spirit.

So who is that lady sitting over there in that cluttered living room, surrounded by piles of newspapers, books read and unread, suitcases still to be unpacked from distant trips, and hungry children asking to be taken out to dinner because, as usual, there isn't any food in the house? That woman in the loose cotton shirt, with the vaguely ethnic kimono jacket over it? The one with her legs crossed on the couch, so you can see her kneesocks—she's kicked off her clogs because she is incapable of keeping her shoes on when she is sitting down (she's also incapable of wearing real grownup shoes, or pantyhose, but never mind that now). That lady knitting along with tight even compulsive little stitches? Well, she is a tight knitter who likes to wear loose clothing.

Whatever strength and security I manage to draw from my tight little stitches (and I really can't loosen up, even if I try—there's no pleasure for me in yarn wound slackly around my left index finger), I don't experience the same reinforcement from sweaters that fit tight to the body. Of course, some of that may be vanity; perhaps if I had a completely different body, I would have a completely different personal aesthetic, and perhaps I would relish the sensation of ribbing slightly stretched, of snug neck and underarms....no, I just can't do it. I conjure that up, even with a highly unlikely fantasy of my new svelte self, and I start to wriggle, if not writhe. I like great sweeping sleeves, with big loose armholes, flowing sweaters and jackets, knitted fabric that can relax and drape rather than stretching or even fitting snugly.

That's who I am, then. That's my personality profile, my own individual blend of what orders my universe and what feels good against my skin. I can't change it, I wouldn't try, and it seems to me a basic and true statement of how I live inside my mind and my body, and then how that mind and body lives in the world. The problem, as any experienced knitter will immediately have detected, is gauge. Or, as Elizabeth Zimmermann would have put it, GAUGE. Let us say, for example, that I am looking over a pattern for a cardigan sweater (I am always drawn to cardigans because, just as I like wearing clogs because the open back gives me that sense that I can always sit down and slip my feet out, I like the feeling that I have an easy way out of any jacket or sweater I happen to be wearing). I automatically go up at least one needle size from the recommended needles; that's the extra I need for being such a tight knitter. Then I make a swatch. Then I start to worry that I will tighten up more and more as I get used to working with the yarn, as I wear that groove into my index finger. So then I plan to make the sweater one size larger than I really need. I cast on, forcing myself to cast on loosely—like many a tight knitter, I have ruined many a project by casting on a miserly inelastic border. I start knitting. I check the gauge again, and begin to worry that what with the larger needles and the too-large size, I have actually committed myself to a garment so improbably oversized that first of all, I will be working on it for the next six months, second of all, I will run out of yarn because the thing is going to be so much bigger than anyone ever imagined, and third of all, if I ever finish it, it will be unwearable, even for someone who likes to wear loose clothing. So, generally, I rip out, rewind my yarn, and decide to cast on for the correct size—but maybe I move up one more needle size, because it seems to me that I'm still creating smaller than ideal stitches for the yarn in question. OK, make another swatch, and now I am definitively over the gauge, so if I just make the sweater in the correct size, it ought to come out a little on the loose side. Cast on—still forcing myself to do it loosely—for the correct size and start to knit. Begin to worry that the "correct size" always feels too small and too tight, and that I was right the first time. And so on.

The end result of all these struggles, as you can probably imagine, is that I make a lot of scarves, many children's sweaters, the occasional shawl, and more than a few hats. For myself, I am in constant search of the right designed-to-be-loose open-in-the-front patterns which will satisfy all my twitches—I'd like colorwork and complexity of pattern but simplicity of drape and construction. I'd like garments I can construct with my painstaking little even stitches, and then wear flowing loosely around me, so that I can take my proper bohemian place in the world, rubbing the groove I have worn in my left index finger.

Acknowledgements & Credits

Two sweaters for my father
PUBLISHED BY XRX BOOKS

PUBLISHER
Alexis Yiorgos Xenakis

MANAGING EDITOR
David Xenakis

EDITOR
Elaine Rowley

EDITORIAL ASSISTANT
Sue Nelson

COPY EDITOR
Holly Brunner

GRAPHIC DESIGNER
Bob Natz

PRODUCTION DIRECTOR & COLOR
SPECIALIST
Dennis Pearson

BOOK PRODUCTION MANAGER
Susan Becker

PRODUCTION
Everett Baker
Nancy Holzer

MIS
Jason Bittner

FIRST PUBLISHED IN USA IN 2004
BY XRX, INC.
COPYRIGHT © 2004 XRX, INC.

All rights reserved.
No part of this publication may be
reproduced, stored in a retrieval system, or
transmitted, in any form or by any means,
electronic, mechanical, photocopying,
recording or otherwise, without the prior
permission of the copyright holder.

ISBN 1-893762-22-X
Produced in Sioux Falls, South Dakota,
by XRX, Inc., PO Box 1525, Sioux Falls,
SD 57101-1525 USA 605.338.2450

My thanks to Nancy Newhouse at the *New York Times*, a wonderful editor who first gave me my chance to write about medicine and then gave me my first chance to write about knitting, and how the two connected. Nancy Thomas encouraged me and brought me into the knitting magazine world, and I have been made truly welcome by the wonderful people at XRX, including Rick Mondragon, Alexis Xenakis, Elaine Rowley, Bob Natz, Susan Becker, and Sue Nelson. My thanks as well to Nicola Earnshaw and June Bridgewater at Rowan. I thank Kaffe Fassett and Brandon Mably for inspiration and good fellowship. No book of knitting essays should be without a yarnshop acknowledgment, and I thank Woolcott in Cambridge, Massachusetts, for years of yarn, knitting advice, and good company. I am grateful to Elaine Markson, for shepherding this book project along. We all need people to knit for, we all need people with whom to talk knitting.

I want to thank my family, Larry, Orlando, Josephine, and Anatol, for putting up with years of sudden emergency yarn shop stops, for waiting patiently while I finish the row—or the sleeve—or the square, for letting me knit for them and for wearing many of my finest—and less fine—creations. Special thanks to Renee Wolff, a superb and enthusiastic knitter, who has kept my children—her grandchildren—supplied with everything from baby blankets to jackets to scarves, and has kept me supplied with knitting conversation, company, and stimulation.

The essays in this book originally appeared in *Knitter's Magazine* and in other publications, sometimes in slightly different form; each source is credited, and permission to reprint is gratefully acknowledged. "The Great Unfinishable" first appeared in *KnitLit Too*, edited by Linda Roghaar and Molly Wolff, published by Three Rivers Press. The expanded version of the essay, "Two Sweaters for My Father," appeared for the first time in *For the Love of Knitting: A Celebration of the Knitter's Art*, edited by Kari Cornell, published by Voyageur Press. The three "Letters from America" originally appeared in separate issues of the *Rowan Newsletter*, Autumn 2003, Spring 2004, and Autumn 2004.

a publication of  BOOKS

Visit us online at www.knittinguniverse.com